The Women's Army Auxiliary Corps in France, 1917–1921

For Mum, Dad and Ian.

In memory of the women who served in the WAAC and QMAAC, especially those who died in the service of their country.

The Women's Army Auxiliary Corps in France, 1917–1921

Women Urgently Wanted

Samantha Philo-Gill

To Simon,

S. Philo-Gill

PEN & SWORD
HISTORY

First published in Great Britain in 2017 by
Pen & Sword History
an imprint of
Pen & Sword Books Ltd
47 Church Street
Barnsley
South Yorkshire
S70 2AS

ISBN 978 1 47383 359 3

A CIP catalogue record for this book is available from the British
Library

Typeset in Ehrhardt by
Mac Style Ltd, Bridlington, East Yorkshire
Printed and bound in the UK by CPI Group (UK) Ltd,
Croydon, CRO 4YY

Pen & Sword Books Ltd incorporates the imprints of Pen & Sword
Archaeology, Atlas, Aviation, Battleground, Discovery, Family
History, History, Maritime, Military, Naval, Politics, Railways,
Select, Transport, True Crime, and Fiction, Frontline Books, Leo
Cooper, Praetorian Press, Seaforth Publishing and Wharncliffe.

For a complete list of Pen & Sword titles please contact
PEN & SWORD BOOKS LIMITED
47 Church Street, Barnsley, South Yorkshire, S70 2AS, England
E-mail: enquiries@pen-and-sword.co.uk
Website: www.pen-and-sword.co.uk

Contents

List of Illustrations

Acknowledgements

I would like to thank the following libraries, archives, museums and organisations for their assistance in the research for this book and for their permission to quote from a selection of resources: Hillingdon Library Service; Brunel University London Library; the National Archives; the National Army Museum; the London Metropolitan Archives; the Commonwealth War Graves Commission; and the Library and Research Room Services, Museum Archive, Documents and Sound Section and Art Section at the Imperial War Museum London and Duxford.

A number of publishers and newspapers have granted me permission to quote from their publications. I would like to thank: James Clarke & Co Ltd; The Permissions Company, Inc., on behalf of the Feminist Press; *The Press and Journal* and *Dundee Evening Telegraph* (DC Thomson & Co Ltd); *Hastings and St. Leonards Observer*, *Yorkshire Evening Post* and *Motherwell Times* (Johnston Press Plc); Times Newspapers Ltd (News UK & Ireland Ltd); and Trinity Mirror Plc for *Manchester Evening News*, *Birmingham Daily Post*, *Liverpool Daily Post and Mercury*, *Liverpool Echo* and *Daily Mirror*.

My thanks also go to Guildford Cathedral for facilitating a very special visit and permitting me to photograph the commemorative window and to reproduce the resulting images in this book.

I am grateful to Birkbeck College, University of London for permitting me to use material from the autobiography and private papers of Dame Helen Gwynne-Vaughan. I would also like to thank Louise McNulty for kindly permitting me to reproduce the photographs of her great-aunt and to quote from her great-grandmother's letter to the Imperial War Museum. My thanks also go to Jessica Bailey for her permission to quote from Dorothy Pickford's letters. I am grateful for the support given to me by the Women's Royal Army Corps Association and their permission to quote from the Old Comrades Association Gazettes.

I would like to thank the Imperial War Museum and Bamforth and Co. Ltd for permission to reproduce a number of images within this book. I am also grateful to Yvonne Milsome for photographing and preparing a number of the images for publication.

I am indebted to my parents and my husband for their support and encouragement during the research and writing of this book.

Timeline

Women's Services Committee appointed	17 November 1916
Lawson Report commissioned	8 December 1916
Women's Services Committee Report	14 December 1916
War Office Conferences	5–15 January 1917
Lawson Report	16 January 1917
War Office Conference	6 February 1917
Appointment of Mona Chalmers Watson (Chief Controller)	February 1917
Appointment of Helen Gwynne-Vaughan (Chief Controller Overseas)	19 February 1917
Inauguration of Women's Branch – AG11	19 February 1917
Official announcement of Corps in press	28 February 1917
Army Council Instruction 537	28 March 1917
First draft enrolled in WAAC	28 March 1917
First draft embarked for France	31 March 1917
General Instructions No 1	1 June 1917
WAAC headquarters established in France (Abbeville)	1 June 1917
Standing Orders	20 June 1917
Army Council Instruction 1069	7 July 1917
Recruitment transferred to Ministry of Labour	August 1917
Transfer of all Women's Legion Cookery Section	September 1917
Appointment of Florence Leach (Chief Controller)	11 February 1918
Commission of Enquiry appointed	11 February 1918
Commission of Enquiry Report	20 March 1918
Michael Offensive	21 March 1918

Corps became Queen Mary's Army Auxiliary Corps	9 April 1918
Georgette Offensive	9 April 1918
Non-fatal attack on Abbeville camp	21–22 May 1918
Fatal attack on Abbeville camp	29–30 May 1918
Formation of Service of Patrols	May 1918
Publication of regulations for the QMAAC	1 June 1918
First draft attached to American Expeditionary Force	11 July 1918
Appointment of Lila Davy (Chief Controller Overseas)	1 September 1918
Armistice	11 November 1918
Visit by Princess Mary	November 1918
Army Council decision to maintain WAAC	March 1919
End of WAAC attachment to American Expeditionary Force	27 June 1919
Peace Treaty	28 June 1919
First draft of demobilised WAAC reached Folkestone	21 September 1919
Closure of WAAC headquarters in France (Wimereux)	31 October 1919
WAAC ceased to exist as organised body	31 December 1919
Old Comrades Association established	December 1919
WAAC disbanded	30 April 1920
St Pol WAAC unit demobilised	27 September 1921
Unveiling of commemorative window in Guildford Cathedral	September 1961
Combined Women's Services Diamond Jubilee Service	3 March 1977
Last WAAC veteran –Ivy Campany – died	19 December 2008
QMAAC Standard laid up in Guildford Cathedral	20 May 2012

Glossary

AAG	Assistant Adjutant General
ACI	Army Council Instruction
AEF	American Expeditionary Force
AG	Adjutant General
AMTD	Advanced Mechanical Transport Depot
ASC	Army Service Corps
ATS	Auxiliary Territorial Service
BRCS	British Red Cross Society
BSM	British School of Motoring
CBE	Commander of the Most Excellent Order of the British Empire
CWGC	Commonwealth War Graves Commission
DBE	Dame Commander of the Order of the British Empire
DORA	Defence of the Realm Act
EFC	Expeditionary Force Canteen
ENSA	Entertainments National Service Association
FANY	First Aid Nursing Yeomanry
GCC	Ground Close Combat
GHQ	General Headquarters
GOC	General Officer Commanding
IWM	Imperial War Museum
QMAAC	Queen Mary's Army Auxiliary Corps
MM	Military Medal
NCO	Non-Commissioned Officer
NUWW	National Union of Women Workers
OBE	Order of the British Empire
OBOS	Overseas Branch of the Ordnance Survey

OCA	Old Comrades Association
SOSBW	Society for Overseas Settlement of British Women
POW	Prisoner of War
PTSD	Post-Traumatic Stress Disorder
RAF	Royal Air Force
RAMC	Royal Army Medical Corps
RFC	Royal Flying Corps
VAD	Voluntary Aid Detachment(s)
YMCA	Young Men's Christian Association
YWCA	Young Women's Christian Association
WAAC	Women's Army Auxiliary Corps
WEC	Women's Emergency Corps
WRAC	Women's Royal Army Corps
WRAF	Women's Royal Air Force
WRNS	Women's Royal Naval Service
WSPU	Women's Social and Political Union
WSWCC	Women's Sick and Wounded Convoy Corps
WVR	Women's Volunteer Reserve
WWS	Women's Work Section
WWSC	Women's Work Sub-Committee

Introduction

Only two books have been written specifically about the Women's Army Auxiliary Corps (WAAC): *Eve in Khaki* by Edith Barton and Marguerite Cody (1918)[1] and *A Short History of the Queen Mary's Army Auxiliary Corps* by Colonel Julia Cowper (1967).[2] Neither of these books have been in print for many years and copies are difficult to obtain. A further two books on women in the British Army include chapters on the WAAC: *The Women's Royal Army Corps* by Shelford Bidwell (1977)[3] and *Women in Khaki: The Story of the British Woman Soldier* by Roy Terry (1988).[4] Each has had an emphasis on different elements of the history of the Corps and used the women's own words to varying degrees.

This book has been written with four objectives. The first is to provide a comprehensive history of the Corps from its design and implementation through to disbandment. The second is to provide social context.

The third is to describe life in the WAAC using the women's oral and written testimonies. In the First World War, there was no one experience for women, no 'everywoman' and this was equally the case for the WAACs. Their subsequent memories, views and opinions were dependent on a range of factors, from their age and social background to their political and religious beliefs.

The final objective is to consider what happened to the women once their services were no longer required and how they have been remembered by the society they served.

On 9 April 1918, Queen Mary was appointed as the Commandant-in-Chief of the Corps, which was re-named Queen Mary's Army Auxiliary Corps (QMAAC). For ease, and due to the fact that the majority of the women continued to refer to themselves as the WAAC, the Corps is mainly referred to as the WAAC throughout this book.

Wherever possible, the date of an event has been included. A key principle in the writing of this book has been to place events in chronological order, both within a chapter and throughout the book. As each chapter has a theme, there is a degree of overlap between some chapters.

The book focuses on the experience of women in France. Many decisions made by the War Office and Treasury affected the Corps at home and in France in different ways.

Chapter 1

Establishment

Working Alongside Men

Throughout history and across the world, war has been, and continues to be, portrayed as a primarily male experience. However, British women travelled overseas to theatres of war as camp followers and nurses in the Napoleonic, Crimean and Boer wars and suffered the same privations as the men for whom they cared. A number of pseudo-military voluntary organisations were established by and for women prior to the First World War. The Women's Sick and Wounded Convoy Corps (WSWCC), Voluntary Aid Detachments (VAD) and First Aid Nursing Yeomanry Corps (FANY) were all established by 1909.

The First World War was the first war in the Western world in which women moved from the private to the public sphere in significant numbers. As it developed into an industrial war, it was clear that women would be required to take on less traditional roles. Men's roles were vacated as increasing numbers of them volunteered or were conscripted, and the war machine needed to be fed with manufactured weapons and ammunition.

In addition, women endeavoured to organise themselves in voluntary organisations along quasi-military lines, for example through the wearing of uniform and establishing rank structures. In August 1914, the Women's Emergency Corps (WEC) was founded and later became the Women's Volunteer Reserve (WVR). The Women's Legion provided cooks and waitresses for the Army at home from 3 August 1915, as well as drivers for the Army Service Corps (ASC) and Royal Flying Corps (RFC) from 1916. The Women's Legion was recognised by an Army Council Instruction (ACI) in February 1916 and they were the first women to officially work alongside the British Army. Women also served as clerks in the War Office.

Devising a Women's Corps

At the end of 1916, Britain was experiencing a manpower shortage as a result of heavy losses during the Battle of the Somme. There was disagreement between government departments (e.g. War Office, Ministry of Munitions and Board of Trade) regarding how the remaining manpower should be employed. The Army Council needed to ensure it was making the most effective use of army resources. This was particularly important if it was to request more men via the Manpower Distribution Board, which had been established independently of competing government departments to determine the distribution of labour. In November 1916, it was the Manpower Distribution Board that recommended to the Army Council that it consider a suggestion made by Katharine Furse (Head of the VAD) that a trained corps of volunteer uniformed women be established to substitute men in subsidiary army services.[1]

On 8 December 1916, the Army Council instructed Lieutenant General Henry Lawson to assist Field Marshall Sir Douglas Haig in reviewing the number and physical categories of men employed out of the fighting area in France. The War Office had already written to Haig on 4 December 1916 to seek his views on recruiting women to work with the Army in France. He responded on 10 December 1916 that he was prepared to accept the principle and that steps were being taken to ascertain the number that could work in the Office of the Director General of Transportation.[2] Sir Eric Geddes, Director General of Transportation in France, was rather more cautious. He was keen for women to substitute men as clerks but believed that, in civil life, ten – twelve per cent more women were required to do the same work as men. He stated that:

They cannot stand the long hours which men will work, nor can they stand times of extreme pressure extending over a period of weeks. Further, the proportion of them who are off work for minor complaints is greater than is the case with men.[3]

He also considered that women clerks were less adaptable and generally less useful than men. He requested an initial ninety-six women and began to arrange their accommodation.

On 17 November 1916, the Minister of Munitions – the Right Hon. Edwin Samuel Montagu – had appointed the Women's Services Committee. It was chaired by Sir George Newman and included Katharine Furse, Lilian Clapham (Board of Trade), Benjamin Seebohm Rowntree (Welfare Dept., Ministry of Munitions) and May Tennant (Welfare Advisor, War Office). The objective of the Committee was to review the supply and organisation of women's services in canteens, hostels, clubs etc. connected with the welfare of munitions workers.[4] The Committee reported on 14 December 1916. Although the focus was on munitions workers, the Committee also provided observations and recommendations on the wider employment of women for war purposes. They were concerned that many women were not usefully employed. This was partly due to a proportion of women being employed in work that was not considered of national importance, but mainly because of a lack of organisation. The Committee acknowledged that there was both a requirement for women to carry out war work (paid or voluntary) and a willingness from women of all classes to be employed. It recommended that a central Board or Committee be established, consisting mainly of women, to enrol, train and place women for state service. The Committee also reported that:

Evidence has been given, both to the effect that large numbers of men, enlisted and otherwise, might be replaced by women in non-combatant positions, and that women under discipline have been able to perform very efficient service in a variety of ways in such occupations.[5]

The report reiterated opinions that Katharine Furse had independently expressed since the beginning of 1916.

Separately, in December 1916, Florence Leach of the Cookery Section of the Women's Legion visited France to see if it could staff Officers Clubs at the army bases, rather than using men from the ASC.

On 5 January 1917, the Adjutant General (AG) at the War Office – Sir Nevil Macready – convened a conference to discuss how women employed by the Army should be organised.[6] Attendees included Florence Leach and Brigadier General (later Sir) Auckland Geddes, Director of Recruitment at the War Office and brother of Sir Eric Geddes. The AG and Auckland Geddes were keen to explore how one simple scheme could be devised which facilitated central control of the women, avoided duplication and ensured that different departments were not competing with each other. No objection was raised to the AG's proposal that the women be treated as an army organisation under the Director General of National Service. Indeed, Florence Leach stated that the women in the Cookery and Household Section of the Women's Legion were 'anxious to be under every sort of Army discipline, and to take the place of soldiers.'[7] It was agreed that the proposed Women's Branch, headed by a Director of Women, would sit under the Director of Organisation in the War Office. The Women's Branch would comprise six sections, each headed by a woman: Motor Section; Canteens; Cookery Section; Clerks; General Service Special Clerks; and Labour (including Ordnance). Florence Leach, who had been recommended as the Head of the Cookery Section, was concerned about the recruitment and 'how [they] are going to tell what sort of characters we are getting.'[8] The AG responded that recruitment would continue along the same lines but with a view to future compulsory service. The latter was never instigated.

Further conferences took place on 10 and 15 January 1917. The discussions went into greater detail with regard to enrolment, medical inspections, pay and the proposed title of the department – the Women's Army Service Department.[9] Meanwhile, ahead of the publication of the Lawson Report, Haig continued to write to the War

Office advising of numbers of women required in various locations, for example 500 women clerks in the Office of the Paymaster-in-Chief to be based in Wimereux.[10] He also requested that an officer of the Postmaster General's Department be sent to France to advise on the capability of the female telegraphers and telephonists already employed in that department in the UK, as well as the instruments that they were able to use, with a view to requesting that a number be transferred to France.

In January 1917, Rachel Crowdy, Principal Commandant of the VAD in France, submitted in writing her views on women's service with the Army.[11] She was in favour of enlistment as she believed that the VADs had already enrolled willing workers and those without ties. She wrote that enlistment would not only secure women who, unless called up, would not want to leave home, but also demonstrate that they were really wanted and prevent them moving from one job to another. Further, she felt that it would control mothers who had already lost husbands and sons and wanted to keep their daughters close. She did not approve of saluting or 'pseudo-men touches' and foresaw that '[c]ertain difficulties may arise, such as drunkenness and immorality, and additional regulations will have to be drawn up to meet these difficulties.'[12] Finally, Rachel Crowdy stated that the women should be recruited from the upper and middle classes.

Lawson published his report on 16 January 1917, in which he recommended that economies be made by the substitution of men by women, juveniles and non-white labour, as well as reorganisation, improved co-ordination and labour-saving devices.[13]

It was in the very first paragraph of the report that he noted that he had emphasised to the heads of services in France that Category A men needed to be replaced by men in lower physical categories or by women. Further, that he had explained the success of substitution by women of men in many areas of employment in England. Lawson stated that it was not only Category A men who could be substituted by women, but also lower category men who may be sent home and consequently release a Category A man. To further press his recommendation regarding substitution by women he argued: '[i]t does not look well, nor is it fair on the men themselves to have quantities of men in khaki doing work which all over England is being done by the other sex.'[14] He also commented that it would have a positive impact on Britain's allies, to see that that men and women were sharing the struggle and everything was being done to increase the number of fighting men.

Lawson reviewed the number of men in the lines of communication and recommended that women could substitute men in the following categories: telegraphists; telephone operators; shorthand writers; typists; clerks; domestic services; store women; postal services; bakers; drivers; packers; counter women; printers and hospital workers. He considered accommodation for the women to be an issue but one that could easily be overcome, for example by building huts or hiring buildings. Lawson believed that the women should be organised in Administrative or Domestic units led by female officers and initially based in Abbeville, Rouen, Le Havre, Dieppe, Étaples, Boulogne and Calais. On 25 February 1917, Haig wrote to the War Office stating that steps had been taken to identify the number of men who could be substituted by women and a further report would be submitted.[15]

The day before the publication of the Lawson Report, General Edward Mabbott Woodward (Director of Organisation at the War Office) wrote to Sir Nevil Macready regarding the establishment of a new War Office Department – the Women's Service Corps.[16] This would require the formation of a new War Office Branch and Woodward proposed that this be named AG11. The Corps would comprise four categories at home and overseas: cooks and waitresses; motor drivers, mechanics and storekeepers; clerks; and those working with Ordnance and the RFC. The first two categories were, at this stage, under the control of the Women's Legion. Woodward advised that the Director of Recruiting at the War Office was ready to assist and that matters of uniform, pay etc. were under consideration. This request was met.

On 26 January 1917, the Women's Interest Committee of the National Union of Women Suffrage Societies wrote to Lord Derby – the Secretary of State for War – regarding the employment of women in the Army. They welcomed the proposal but believed that recruitment and control of women, particularly overseas, should be in the hands of women. They recommended that a Board be established which had experience in dealing with the organisation of large numbers of women.[17]

At the end of January 1917, after the publication of the Lawson Report, Sir Nevil Macready wrote to Lord Derby. He stated that the War Office was unlikely to fully accept Lawson's recommendation that 12,100 women be employed in France but women 'will be largely made use of'.[18] He referred to an 'agitation which is being engineered by those who run various women's organisations throughout the country'[19] but that, in his opinion, women employed by the Army should remain distinct from other women's organisations. He was concerned that: '[i]f we once admit outside interference, jealousy will be created among the various organisations, and I feel sure there will be no peace.'[20] He went on to propose the organisational structure previously set out by Woodward and although recommending that the heads of women's organisations be consulted, he was not desirous of their advice once the scheme was launched.

Sir Reginald Brade, Permanent Under-Secretary of State for War, responded to Sir Nevil Macready on behalf of the Secretary of State. He agreed with the proposals and that, although ladies interested in war work should be consulted as to the heads of section of the Women's Branch and the general rules of the scheme, outside interference should be resisted.[21] He was content that women from the Women's Legion be considered for the posts of section heads. Further, the Secretary of State did not believe that women should be fully enlisted.

At the beginning of February 1917, two women wrote to the War Office with their views on organisation of women in the Army: Barbara Marion Craster, who later joined the Women's Royal Naval Service (WRNS); and Katharine Furse. The latter wrote a very detailed letter in which she suggested collectively naming the women the 'Queen's Women' or 'Queen Mary's Imperial Women' and to use the head of Joan of Arc as their emblem.[22] Like Rachel Crowdy, her colleague in the VAD, Katherine Furse was most concerned about the potential behaviour of the women. She wrote that:

> The women would undoubtedly become engaged both to British and French men. They should not be allowed to marry within six months of enlisting, and should then be discharged. Unmarried mothers, or those about to become so, must be discharged. They should not, however, be lost sight of, but their names and home addresses should be given to some competent organisation with a view to their being properly cared for. As the responsibility for this will be for the men as well as the women, some definite action should be decided upon, and permitting marriage will be the only solution.[23]

Given that this approach had not been taken for members of the VAD, who were drawn from the upper classes, her view may have been based on an assumption that the women to be employed by the Army would be of a lower social class, of which she held a rather low opinion. Katharine Furse believed that if Queen Mary took an interest in the women, they would not disgrace her.

The need for women in France continued and Sir Eric Geddes wrote to the AG at the War Office that he could substitute 134 men with 161 well-trained female clerks if suitable accommodation could be found.[24]

Creation of the WAAC

It was at this point that Auckland Geddes contacted his sister, Dr Alexandra Mary Chalmers Watson, for assistance. Known as Mona, she was 44 years old and was the first woman to graduate as a Doctor of Medicine from the University of Edinburgh. She came from a family of distinguished medical women. Her aunt, Dr Elizabeth Garrett Anderson, was the first female medical doctor in Britain. Mona's cousin, Dr Louisa Garrett Anderson, co-founded the military hospital in Endell Street, London which was staffed by women of the Women's

Hospital Corps. Chalmers Watson later explained that she received a summons to attend a meeting in London but that she did not know what it was about. She met Auckland Geddes a couple of days before the meeting and he provided her with a copy of the Lawson Report.[25]

The Secretary of State for War had recommended that he should host a conference with the leaders of women's organisations on the 30 January 1917. Due to his health it was postponed until 6 February 1917. As well as War Office representatives, attendees included: the Marchioness of Londonderry (WVR); Florence Leach; Christabel Ellis (Women's Legion); Katharine Furse; Lilian Clapham; Dr Louisa Garrett Anderson; Mrs Maxwell; May Tennant; and Violet Markham. The latter two women had recently been appointed Director and Assistant Director respectively of the Women's Section of the Department of National Service. Chalmers Watson was also present at the meeting. The Secretary of State explained that 12,000 women would take up work in France in various sections headed by women and that all would be controlled by the Army. A number of elements were discussed and it was agreed that: women should indeed control the sections; the women should be housed together rather than billeted; decisions on clothing and exercise be made by the section heads; the women should be paid on the same basis as the men they replaced; and they should not be accepted if they had dependents. The Secretary of State noted that he could not guarantee that the women at officer grade would be awarded that rank.[26]

Chalmers Watson complained to Auckland Geddes that the meeting had been unsatisfactory and he suggested that she meet privately with the AG.[27] A meeting subsequently took place at which Sir Nevil Macready asked for Chalmers Watson's opinion of the women who had attended the conference on 6 February 1917. Chalmers Watson considered that 'there were two types: the anti–suffrage woman who believed in getting her way by cajolery and the suffrage type of professional worker.'[28] The AG stated that he preferred the latter and asked for her views on the organisation of women working in the Army.

She provided him with some rough notes that she had made with her cousin Dr Louisa Garrett Anderson.

A couple of days later, the AG asked Chalmers Watson if she would be the head of the scheme if it was approved by the Secretary of State. He explained that "'Lord Derby wishes a lady of title. I want a working woman.'"[29] Chalmers Watson, however, required time to consider the offer because of her professional commitments in Scotland, as well as the needs of her young family. When they met again, she explained that due to her family, she did not want to work in France and suggested that a deputy be appointed. The AG appointed her Chief Controller and gave her permission to seek a deputy to serve as Controller in France.

Dr Louisa Garrett Anderson was aware of Mona's situation and introduced her to her friend, Dr Helen Gwynne-Vaughan, with whom she had established the University of London Suffrage Society before the war. Gwynne-Vaughan was 38 years old and had been widowed in September 1915. She was head of the Department of Botany at Birkbeck College, University of London. As a consequence of studying medical bacteriology, she had considered war service in a hospital or mobile laboratory behind the front line.

On 11 February 1917, Chalmers Watson and Gwynne-Vaughan met for the first time. Gwynne-Vaughan was thrilled at the meeting and in her autobiography, *Service with the Army*,[30] she wrote that the plans for the women's corps were 'like the realization of a dream'.[31] It is probable that her eagerness to join stemmed from the fact that she had been brought up in an army family. Her father, who had died when she was 5 years old, was an officer in the Scots Guards and her grandfather, stepfather and an uncle had also served in the Army. Gwynne-Vaughan appreciated the military way of life. The two women met again the following day to discuss the matter further. Various secondary sources conclude that the women differed in terms of personality but got on well with each other.[32] In a letter from Gwynne-Vaughan to Chalmers Watson when the latter later resigned from the Corps, she wrote that '[f]or myself I can look back upon much unofficial friendliness and help over and above our official relation – I hope the former will carry on.'[33] This suggests a genuine friendship existed between the two women.

Gwynne-Vaughan was interviewed on 13 February 1917 by Sir Nevil Macready for the post of Controller in France. It transpired that although they had not met, he had been Adjutant of the Gordon Highlanders when she 'came out' at their ball in Aberdeen in 1896. Although this would have provided him with a sense of the type of woman that he was interviewing, he was less interested in appointing a woman of title and more in a professional working woman. Gwynne-Vaughan was well suited to the role as she was a woman of social standing and a professional working woman, as well as the daughter of an army family. Although Chalmers Watson and Gwynne-Vaughan were both from the upper-middle class, they had experience of working with young working class women. At the interview, Gwynne-Vaughan asked to be sent to France even if she was not appointed Chalmers Watson's deputy and she believed that this was one of the reasons why she was subsequently appointed Chief Controller (Overseas) six days later.

In February 1917, Florence Leach was appointed as Controller of Cooks and began to identify individuals who would transfer from the Women's Legion Cookery Section to serve in the new Corps in France.

Lawson subsequently submitted a continuation to his report on 18 February 1917 after visiting other places on the lines of communication and the armies at the behest of Haig. This resulted in the addition of St Omer and Paris, as well as General Headquarters (GHQ) to the list of locations where women were required.

On 19 February 1917, the Women's Branch, known as AG11, within the AG's Department of the War Office, was officially inaugurated and headed by Assistant Adjutant General (AAG), Lieutenant Colonel James Leigh-Wood. Gwynne-Vaughan had met the latter when she was interviewed by Sir Nevil Macready. AG11 was based at Devonshire House, Piccadilly, London, alongside the headquarters of the VAD. Shortly afterwards, Chalmers Watson and Gwynne-Vaughan were informed that the Corps had been named the Women's Army Auxiliary Corps.

Gwynne-Vaughan discovered that in the order announcing both her and Chalmers Watson's appointments, they were referred to as Chief Women's Controllers. Gwynne-Vaughan was unimpressed that she was required to announce her gender but did not believe that the Army Council would change the title. However, by contacting Sir Nevil Macready and advising that she did not want to be known as the Chief W.C. she successfully managed to influence a change in the title to Chief Controller.

Implementation of the WAAC

Gwynne-Vaughan and Chalmers Watson left for France on 25 February 1917 with Leigh-Wood. They met with Chalmers Watson's brother – Sir Eric Geddes – to discuss accommodation for the WAAC clerks that he had requested. As a result of their meeting, Chalmers Watson returned early to the UK to progress matters. Gwynne-Vaughan kept a diary during the rest of her stay in France in which she recorded details of her visits to GHQ, Wimereux, Calais, Étaples, Le Touquet, Abbeville, Le Havre and Rouen.[34] She and Leigh-Wood met with the Army to discuss accommodation, washing and laundry facilities, the system of drawing rations, pay and the size of drafts required from the UK. They reviewed the female carpenters employed by Walter Tarrant to construct the wooden prefabricated Tarrant hut, as well as visiting their living accommodation. Gwynne-Vaughan recalled that on their travels, she asked Leigh-Wood what his wife thought about the Corps. His response was that his wife was a truly feminine woman. Gwynne-Vaughan considered that this reflected a view held by many, that there was something not quite nice about the Corps.[35]

On 25 February 1917, Haig replied to the War Office with his initial response to the full Lawson Report.[36] He agreed with Lawson that the women should be organised into units under female officers and recommended not less than one officer and twenty women per unit. He provided an appendix showing how many women clerks and domestics were required and in which location, as well as suggestions regarding potential accommodation. He also recommended that consideration be given to sending women out as drivers, telegraphists, telephonists and cleaners. He agreed with Lawson that women could not be used in the Royal Army Medical Corps (RAMC) with the armies due to the physical nature of the work, for example lifting men on stretchers. Three days later, Haig wrote to the War Office that he urgently required women clerks at Boulogne to censor letters written by German prisoners of war (POWs).

By this stage, representatives of the Postmaster General had visited France and completed their report. They concluded that there would be no serious difficulty in staffing Telephone and Telegraph Offices of the Signal Service at Boulogne, Étaples, GHQ, Abbeville, Dieppe, Le Havre and Rouen with 574 women.[37]

On 11 March 1917, Haig wrote again to the War Office, this time with his detailed response to the Lawson Report.[38] He agreed where women could be employed but also included references to perceived limitations of women in certain categories of work. For example, that as cooks they would not be able to lift carcasses of beef, as postal workers they would be slow to acquire the requisite knowledge and that they could not be storekeepers for men's clothing as the latter would need to change in front of them. This was balanced by positive observations, for example that women were skilled in motor car driving and running repairs. He expressed concerns about the accommodation of women in France, particularly in relation to the men. He noted that the General Officer Commanding (GOC) Lines of Communication Area believed that male reinforcements at the army bases, including many who had come direct from the Front, were less controlled than at home and therefore there was a likelihood of the 'sex difficulty' at these locations. Haig considered there to be a further issue at the bases and lines of communication in terms of the mixing of non-white labour with women and recommended white guards for the latter. This reflects the prevailing attitudes regarding women and ethnic minorities at that time. Finally, Haig stated that the women:

> must be prepared to experience a certain degree of bodily discomfort, both in offices and in their dwellings, to which they will be unaccustomed: they must be disciplined: they may be called upon in times of stress to perform long hours of duty: they must realize that there are few or no distractions, and that no one in this country has time for anything but work.[39]

Gwynne-Vaughan had returned to the UK on 4 March 1917 to work with Chalmers Watson on the organisation of the Corps. Her stay was brief and she left for France again on 19 March 1917, where she continued to review accommodation and address issues such as discipline. Nine days after her return, ACI 537 was published which approved the 'employment of women at the Base and on the Lines of Communication abroad.'[40]

The objective of the WAAC was to achieve substitution i.e. replace men at the bases and in the lines of communication, as well as at home. No woman was to be employed unless a soldier was released for combat. They were to be in an auxiliary role thereby facilitating what was perceived to be the more important work of the men. Later, in March 1918, the American journalist and author Fryniwyd Tennyson Jesse observed that:

> Every WAAC who goes to France is like the pawn who attains the top of the chessboard and is exchanged for a more valuable piece. She sends a fighting man to his job by taking on the jobs that are really a woman's after all. For is it not woman's earliest job to look after man?[41]

This secondary role was further emphasised by dilution – an arrangement whereby more than one woman was used to carry out a role formerly filled by one man. This was already taking place in industry in the UK due to concerns around the de-skilling of men's jobs, reduced pay and the maintenance of production levels. When the employment of women in France was initially proposed, Haig suggested using dilution and recommended a ratio of 200 women to replace 134 men as clerks and in domestic services.[42] Dilution was indeed utilised in the subsequent establishment of the Corps.

Rank, Grade and Status

In March 1917, there was some debate about the wearing of badges that denoted rank. The recommendation from Chalmers Watson and Gwynne-Vaughan was that military rank badges (i.e. crown and star) should be worn by all women holding the equivalent to commissioned rank, as well as rank rings on tunic sleeves.[43] Indeed, Gwynne-Vaughan wore the rank badges equivalent to a lieutenant colonel when she first went to France. On 22 March 1917, Gwynne-Vaughan met with the AG (Expeditionary Force) – Lieutenant General George Henry Fowke – at GHQ in France. He approved of her rank badges and also approved of saluting as long as it was in a simple form and, with Lieutenant Colonel Whitehead of the AG's Office, communicated this to the War Office.[44]

On 31 March 1917, Gwynne-Vaughan recorded in her diary that she had visited GHQ, France and had been informed that the matter of the status of officers, badges and saluting had been put up to the War Office. She observed that in the meantime, the WAAC had continued to take salutes.[45] On the same day she met with Lawson, who shared with her Haig's response to his report. Gwynne-Vaughan focused on the reference to the potential 'sex difficulty' at the army bases. In response she emphasised to Lawson the consequent 'importance of official rank and treatment, saluting, forms of respect etc' and that the AG and Whitehead were in favour of her approach.[46] Lawson agreed to support her in the matter with the War Office and she concluded that he was most helpful.

The proposals regarding rank badges were almost submitted to the king for approval at the end of March 1917 but were then subject to reconsideration. Gwynne-Vaughan had believed that the AG supported her. However, he wrote to the War Office in April 1917 with concerns that if the women wore military rank badges they would be saluted but as they did not hold commissions, they should not be and, therefore, it would be an unlawful command to order that they be saluted. He recommended that consideration be given to badges that could not be confused with those of the Army.[47]

Although a number of decisions had been made at the conference on 6 February 1917, the status of the Corps and the related matters of pay and rank were the subject of prolonged discussions within the War Office. The Finance Branch of the War Office objected to the proposal that women should be treated as soldiers and paid the same as the men, thereby increasing costs and promoting equal pay, which was not the practice among government departments. Chalmers Watson wrote to Gwynne-Vaughan on 12 April 1917 that all efforts were being made to ensure that the Corps was a civilian organisation and confided in her that she considered that an Act of Parliament should be obtained so that women could be enlisted rather than enrolled. Gwynne-Vaughan replied in agreement that the Corps should follow the pattern of army organisation and use the same badges of rank. She was also keen on saluting between the Corps and the Army in order to instil discipline and encourage the Army to see them as clerks, drivers etc. and not as women.

In the same month, the proposal to issue women with rank badges made up of the rather feminine emblems of the rose and fleur-de-lis was agreed by the Secretary of State for War. Gwynne-Vaughan received a letter from Chalmers Watson instructing her to remove her military rank badges. She initially refused and asked Fowke's permission to retain them, but he denied her request.

Gwynne-Vaughan recorded in her diary that the women were to begin saluting immediately, however officials were not to initiate salutes but return them.[48] Saluting was not officially sanctioned but did take place among the women in France.

In April 1917, a compromise was reached with regard to the organisation of the Corps. It would not be integrated into the Army but be organised along the same lines. In France, the WAAC came under the Army Act s.176 (10) which applied to 'all persons not otherwise subject to military law who are followers of or accompany His Majesty's troops, or any portion thereof, when employed in active service.'[49] On occasion, this led to them being referred to as camp followers. The WAACs serving in the UK were subject to civilian law.

The women did not attain a rank but rather a grade. There were no officers in the WAAC. The King's Commission was only available to men. Officer equivalents in the WAAC were referred to collectively as officials and included at home and overseas: chief controller; deputy chief controller; assistant chief controller; area controller; controller; deputy controller; assistant controller; unit administrator; deputy administrator; and assistant administrator. The other grades were referred to as members. The equivalent to non–commissioned officers (NCOs) were forewomen and assistant forewomen. The lower grades were known as workers. Promotion was rare and was generally from worker to forewoman rather than from worker to official. 'Ma'am' was the term used to address seniors.

During these first few months, there was considerable emphasis on the fact that the women in the WAAC did not hold military status and did not have equal status with men. On 21 April 1917, Gwynne-Vaughan was ordered to GHQ in Montreuil and met with Sir Nevil Macready, who had travelled out to France. At the meeting, she was reminded of the civilian status of the WAAC. She wrote in her diary that:

The interview was long and not very satisfactory. The use of the word officer in relation to the WAAC was strongly objected to. Saluting on either side cannot be required and is therefore a mere amenity, but was not disallowed. Gazetting is certain, statement of equivalent rank doubtful, permission to indent apparently to begin. ... Badges probably to be allowed to continue. ... Questions on minor points of general internal discipline are to be put up to Mrs Watson and AG not to be troubled.[50]

The civilian status of the Corps, subsequently decreed by the Secretary of State for War, meant that women in the WAAC were not enlisted but enrolled.

In her autobiography, Gwynne-Vaughan considered that in retrospect, Sir Nevil Macready's severe tone might actually have meant that he was in agreement with her but was unable to admit it. She did not know that Sir Nevil Macready, after visiting the WAAC in France, did indeed feel that the Corps should be a military rather than civilian organisation, albeit the Secretary of State had made the decision otherwise. During May 1917, Sir Nevil Macready wrote to the Financial Secretary to the War Office, Henry William Forster, that:

> Members of the WAAC will be working in very close touch with the Army formations, and arrangements which most nearly conform will cause least difficulty. If you agree we might discuss with the S of S. The matter is very urgent, as the whole business is held up till we can get out our ACI.[51]

The short response from the Secretary of State was that the WAAC would remain civilian and the ACI was to be put out.

During May 1917, discussions about pay were still ongoing at the War Office between the Director of Financial Services, the AG and the Director of Organisation, to the point where the latter complained about the amount of time being wasted and insisted that somebody with the authority to make financial decisions meet with him at his office.[52]

The king approved the rank (or grade) badges on 21 May 1917. The chief controllers initially wore one fleur-de-lis and one rose but this was changed to one fleur-de-lis and two roses. Deputy controllers wore a fleur-de-lis and later a rose was added. Unit administrators wore three roses, deputy administrators two roses and assistant administrators one rose. Forewomen wore a rose within a laurel wreath and assistant forewomen a laurel wreath. The rank (or grade) badges were initially embroidered due to a metal shortage but later produced in metal.

On 25 May 1917, the Secretary of State convened a conference attended by, among others, Sir Nevil Macready and the Financial Secretary to the War Office. It was agreed that all WAACs were to be enrolled and uniformed. Pay was to be on a yearly or weekly rate, with no overtime and 14/- deducted for board and lodging. There was no agreed number of hours worked per week but forty-eight hours a week would be used for the purposes of calculations. The WAAC would also be extended to include service at home.[53]

On 29 May 1917,[54] Colonel J.B. Wroughton of the AG's Office visited Gwynne-Vaughan at Abbeville and gave her advanced sight of the Corps regulations written by the War Office.[55] Gwynne-Vaughan considered that the latter was an uncomfortable document because it 'forbade them to "loiter" outside camps and barracks and which used the discouraging word "must", which suggests coercion, instead of "will", which implies ready obedience.'[56] She readily agreed to Wroughton's suggestion that they re-write it, which they did two days later with the assistance of Whitehead and others in the AG's Office. The resulting regulations, referred to as General Instructions No 1, were signed by Fowke, printed that night and issued on 1 June 1917. They superseded the regulations issued by the War Office, as these did not officially arrive in France until a few days later.

In June 1917, Gwynne-Vaughan drafted Standing Orders for the Corps, which were issued at a conference of administrators held in Boulogne on 20 June 1917. Whereas General Instructions No 1 set out the fit between the WAAC and the Army, the Standing Orders allowed Gwynne-Vaughan to set out the detail of how the WAAC should operate internally. It also included reference to behaviour, stating that:

> The greatest discretion both of behaviour and manner is required on Active Service and it is to be remembered that the Corps is liable to criticism through the unwisdom or even the carelessness

of an individual. These facts are to be borne in mind by all grades when on duty and whenever they appear in public.[57]

In June 1917, Edith Pratt arrived in France as the Deputy Chief Controller. She had previously been a Woman Inspector of Munitions Factories and had received an Order of the British Empire (OBE) for her work. She consequently wore a purple ribbon on her uniform, which led to amusing comments from army officers about her winning the Victoria Cross. In the same month, Chalmers Watson and Florence Leach visited Gwynne-Vaughan in France. Chalmers Watson, who had been concerned with Gwynne-Vaughan's militaristic approach, was satisfied with what she saw of the newly established Corps during her ten-day visit. On her return to the UK, Chalmers Watson decided to send Gwynne-Vaughan's younger sister – Kathleen Pratt-Barlow – to France as an assistant administrator. Gwynne-Vaughan believed that she did this because she perceived her job to be a lonely one and that she would benefit from the company of someone who was able to be frank with her.

On 7 July 1917, ACI 1069 was published which provided the formal basis for the WAAC and approved of the service of the WAAC at home, as well as overseas. It stated that the Military Cookery and Motor Transport Sections of the Women's Legion would gradually be absorbed into the WAAC. They were invited to enrol in the WAAC and undergo a medical examination. ACI 1069 was considerably more detailed than ACI 537 and provided a firm foundation for the Corps for the following four years.

Chapter 2

Preparation

Enrolment and Training

On 20 February 1917, the British press reported that a scheme had been devised whereby women would be substituted for men in the Army where possible, both at home and overseas. The papers stated that a new War Office Branch – AG11 – had been established at Devonshire House, but no other details were known and a statement would be made in due course.

A week later, articles were published in British national newspapers officially announcing that women were to be employed with the Army behind the lines in France. They set out detailed terms and conditions of service, as well as the six categories of work (including Miscellaneous) that would be available and the rates of pay. For overseas service, women were required to be over 20 and under 40 and be British subjects. Women in government employment or in essential occupations were asked not to apply. The War Office instructed that if any woman in army or War Office employment did apply for the WAAC, they should not be selected without reference to the War Office.[1]

At this time, Chalmers Watson, Gwynne-Vaughan and Leigh-Wood were still in France reviewing arrangements, including accommodation. Further, the number of women required was yet to be determined. Interested women were, therefore, requested to make a preliminary offer of service using a form available from National Service headquarters at St Ermin's Hotel, London. The form included questions regarding the women's age, marital status, dependents, nationality and the nationality of their parents. They were also asked to confirm their understanding that they would be subject to certain sections of the Army Act. The emphasis was on service in France but women were also required for service at home, and those who had a preference were to declare it. The process did not apply to female telegraphists and telephonists as they were already employed as civil servants and their offer of service was progressed through internal civil service channels, although they were required to undergo a medical examination. They could only volunteer for service overseas as the requirement for telegraphists and telephonists was in France rather than at home. A number of these women were also given training in postal sorting.

By the beginning of March 1917 the WAAC was oversubscribed, with approximately 16,000 women having expressed an interest in joining the Corps. On 5 March 1917, the General Secretary of the National Service Department wrote to the War Office that the Director, Neville Chamberlain, required that immediate steps be taken to deal with the number of applications. His concern was that many were from women in government posts and he did not want unrest among them. Further, that the length of time between application and a response may lead to criticism.[2] On the same day, after their return from France, Chalmers Watson and Leigh-Wood met with Lilian Clapham of the National Service Department to discuss recruitment. Chalmers Watson estimated that 2,430 clerical workers were needed in France, but in order to effectively train the women and find them accommodation they initially requested only 200.[3] The National Service Department was concerned at the inefficiency of processing 16,000 applications for 200 posts. A key issue was that the newspaper articles published on 28 February 1917 had stated that there were six categories of work available, but the War Office was only considering clerical workers at this point due to a lack of accommodation. As a result, applications were temporarily suspended and of those who had already applied, only those living in London would be enrolled initially, as this was the location of the first WAAC depot. In the meantime, AG11 wrote to various commanders in France requesting details of how many women they could employ.[4]

The first women ready to be enrolled in the WAAC did not come from the pool of volunteers, rather they were transferred from the Women's Legion. In March 1917, a number were sent to the first WAAC depots that were established at both a Church Army hostel on the Harrow Road, London and Ingram House in Stockwell, London.

Following publication of ACI 537 on 28 March 1917, the first draft of WAACs was enrolled – fifteen women from the Women's Legion led by May Anderson Finlay. As more women were selected for enrolment, from the Women's Legion and the pool of volunteers, a further depot opened at the Connaught Club in April 1917. This had been a men's club and initially the women remained on the top floor. Gradually, the men evacuated until the WAAC was the sole occupier.

At the beginning of April 1917, the National Service Department expressed concern to the War Office that the pool of potential recruits in the London area was diminishing. Although 1,322 applications had been received in the London area for clerical work, 376 had been disqualified and 361 worked either in government or essential occupations. The National Service Department requested that recruitment in other regions be considered or the regular supply of recruits to France would be delayed. They also requested that government departments be asked to release women for service as clerks in France.[5] As a result, Selection Boards were held in Edinburgh and Birmingham by the end of April 1917.

Recruitment was also hampered by the fact that many of the women, who had initially expressed an interest in the WAAC but had not been subsequently contacted, had found other employment.

In May 1917, articles were once again in the papers, recruiting for the WAAC. By this time, a clearly defined enrolment process was in place. This was the result of some considerable discussion between the National Service Department, the Ministry of Labour and the War Office.[6] It was agreed that the National Service Department was responsible for finding the number of women required and carrying out an initial sift to ascertain their suitability and character. Assistance was available from the Ministry of Labour if required.

First, applications were made in writing using a National Service Department form, which was available by post, at Employment Exchanges or specific recruitment locations, for example the Mansion House in London.

Second, the women received papers requesting their attendance at Selection Boards at various locations across the country, including London, Edinburgh, Bristol, Birmingham, Manchester and Leeds. The Selection Board comprised representatives from the National Service Department, AG11, the Employment Department of the Ministry of Labour and the recruiting officer. The War Office was ultimately responsible for the final selection. The women attended a Medical Board on the same day and the medical examinations were carried out by female doctors. Elsie Cooper, who was selected and became a worker at the depot in Étaples, remembered the medical examination as 'most embarrassing, I'd never had such a medical examination, even down to your fingers.'[7] Women were asked not to serve notice to their employers until they were informed whether or not they had been successful. The War Office would not hold a Selection Board for less than two days and as 120 women were interviewed each day, the National Service Department waited until 250 applications had been received before convening a Board.[8]

Third, if successful, the women received a letter stating that they had been accepted and providing instructions on which train take to reach their allocated depot. There could be significant delays for the women between attendance at the Selection Board and being notified of the result.

In September 1917, the overseas depot was temporarily established in Warrior Square, St Leonards-on-Sea in Sussex. The Corps occupied sixteen houses and the women ate their meals in a disused theatre. Gwynne-Vaughan recalled that the members ate off long tables erected in the pit and stalls, while the tables for the officials were placed on the stage. Further, the quartermistress used the dressing rooms as store rooms.[9]

In December 1917, the overseas depot was established on a permanent basis at the Hotel Metropole, Folkestone in Kent, which could house 1,200 women. Prior to the war, the luxurious hotel had been a fashionable destination for wealthy visitors to the town. This location was far more suitable for moving WAAC units across to Boulogne. An administrator and her staff, which included a quartermistress and a medical officer, ran the depot. The first administrator was May Margaret Stevenson, followed by Blanche Ireland and Henrietta Carlisle. The local population was initially wary of the women. Gwynne-Vaughan later wrote that the Town Commandant:

> was horrified at the idea of so many women going into the town and tried to insist on them not being allowed out after 1 o'clock mid day. We would not agree but said the majority would be in after 6 pm. And only those on a late pass would be out after that time. After six weeks he called to congratulate us on the discipline which we were able to maintain.[10]

She did, however, also remember the evening that 250 Americans came up the drive wanting to celebrate their last night before embarking for France. The WAACs apparently forgot the need to maintain the blackout and leaned out of their windows to enjoy the fun.[11] The locals took the women to their hearts and they were invited to participate in a sports day, for which local businessmen contributed prizes. The first women to leave the Hotel Metropole for France in December 1917 marched down Slope Road, which is now known as the Road of Remembrance, to the harbour and were cheered by the townspeople.

A number of women were alternatively sent to Star Hill Barracks in Farnborough, Surrey. The building that they occupied was formerly Hillside Convent College, which was a day and boarding school. The War Office had commandeered the building in 1915 and the nuns were relocated to nearby Sycamore House. An RFC, latterly Royal Air Force (RAF), base was located next to Star Hill Barracks and the women could hear the testing of engines during the night.

The women stayed at their depots for two to four weeks. While there, they underwent roll call, physical training, route marches and drill. Ruby Ord, who had previously been a suffragette and member of the WVR, enrolled as a clerk. She described the experience of marching and drill in less than positive tones:

It was awful … we had to get up at about 0600 and do PT and go for a march. We were drilled in the square and were the laughing stock of all the men, of course, which was absurd because none of us had ever done this sort of drill that the army does.[12]

They had lectures on a variety of subjects including hygiene, venereal disease and mixing with men. The women also received their vaccinations and inoculations for smallpox and typhoid at the depots and this often resulted in many of the women becoming unwell. Elizabeth Johnston, a telephonist, wrote home that:

Most of the girls succumb to low spirits and depression and quite a number have to go to hospital. We have 48 hours respite from drill, etc., and if we choose we can remain in bed, but it isn't advisable. There you nurse your pain and are alive to every little twinge, in fact, those who remain in bed become worse. The plan is to get up, and crawl, if you can't walk.[13]

At Folkestone, the women spent their spare time relaxing in what had been the Palm Room at the hotel. They were permitted to hold concerts, which men could attend with written permission from the administrator.

Junior officials had further lectures on specific functions provided by the WAAC, followed by an examination and a fortnight attachment to a unit based in the UK.

Not all the women managed to reach the end of their training. There were those from more privileged backgrounds who found it difficult to adjust to the basic army life. Others did not readily adapt to the lack of freedom or became homesick. Elsie Cooper noted that:

> Some of them, like myself, were quite alright and some of them went home before the end of the training. There was an RAF camp next door and sometimes they invited us to concerts and of course they used to sing songs, "God send you back to me" and all these kind of things and the next morning the girls were off home … homesick …[14]

An army general officer attended the depot to complete enrolment and take the oath as follows:

> I swear by Almighty God, that I will be faithful and bear true Allegiance to His Majesty King George the Fifth, His Heirs and Successors, and that I will, as in duty bound, honestly and faithfully serve His Majesty, His Heirs and Successors, and will observe and obey all orders of His Majesty, His Heirs and Successors, and of the Generals and Officers set over me. So help me God.[15]

The women were enrolled for one year or the duration of the war, whichever was the longest. The women signed an enrolment form in which they agreed to fulfil the Corps rules and regulations, work wherever and in whatever work was requested and be discharged in the case of misconduct or serious breach of regulations. Each was given a regimental number and an identity disc.

ACI 1069 required women already in the WAAC to re-enrol but they did not need to undergo another medical examination. The new rates of pay and conditions in ACI 1069 only applied to those women who re-enrolled. The majority did re-enrol and in some cases the details were recorded in the Corps War Diaries. The Assistant Controller for GHQ 1st Echelon wrote in the War Diary that she was concerned that the ACI would cause complications regarding the pay of women who were already enrolled. She later organised a meeting of representatives of the unit to explain the detail of ACI 1069. She noted that all preferred to stay under ACI 537 due to the impact on their pay.[16] A minority of the WAACs initially resisted and Gwynne-Vaughan considered the reasons to be a perceived loss of both pay and the credit of their early membership. Further, that the women found it a less military affair in comparison to the previous enrolment as they were no longer required to take an oath. Many of those who initially resisted were encouraged to re-enrol in October 1917, when it was announced that those who were still under ACI 537 would not be promoted. The War Diary for GHQ 2nd Echelon records a re-enrolment under ACI 1069 as late as February 1918.[17]

Uniform

For the women, one of the most important events that took place at the depot was the issuing of uniform prior to embarkation for France.

The WAAC uniform was not designed and produced in time for the first draft of women but as they were from the Women's Legion they already had a uniform. Subsequent volunteers who were not from the Women's Legion were required to obtain a uniform from Selfridges until such time as the WAAC uniform was available for issue.

During March 1917 there was much debate between Chalmers Watson, Gwynne-Vaughan and the War Office regarding the uniform. As stated in Chapter 1, much of the discussion was around the extent of the militaristic appearance of the civilian Corps. Lawson had recommended in his 1916 report that the women's uniform should not be khaki but possibly blue[18], but in the end khaki, proposed by Chalmers Watson and Gwynne-Vaughan, was chosen.[19]

The women were given a uniform allowance of £4 at the beginning of their service, followed by a further £1 after six months. Subsequent allowances were provided throughout their remaining service. The allowance was slightly higher for those in the Motor Transport Section. The allowances were credited to the women, the articles of clothing charged against them and any balance paid to the women at the end of their service.

Officials wore a khaki skirt with side pockets, a coat fastened with a cloth belt with two buttons, and a khaki shirt and tie. The pattern was procured from Marshall and Snelgrove's. The jacket had oxidised or leather buttons with the Royal Arms (later bronze with the Corps badge) and side, rather than breast, pockets so as not to accentuate the bust.

Members had one coat frock made of khaki gabardine with two pockets on the skirt and a khaki belt with a removable middle section fastened by buttons. The buttons were not brass but leather or composition material. The worker's coat frocks had a detachable washable brown collar (three issued) and the forewomen's collars were white. Drivers, however, wore a tunic and skirt.

The cloth khaki shoulder straps had a 'WAAC' or 'QMAAC' title (originally embroidered in buff due to a metal shortage but later in metal) and a different coloured insert. The colour was dependent on either grade (blue for controllers, green for recruiting controllers and orange for administrators) or the section that the woman worked in (brown for Clerical, claret for Motor Drivers, red for Household and purple for Mechanical and Miscellaneous).

The women were also issued with two pairs of overalls, one khaki overcoat similar to the men's greatcoat, one pair of brown leather laced shoes, two pairs of khaki woollen stockings (supplied twice a year) and one pair of waterproof gaiters.

Finally, they were provided with a hat: round brown felt for workers and khaki peaked for officials. The brown felt was later changed to khaki. The Corps badge – bronze for officials and gilding-metal for members – was attached to the front, with a coloured felt backing that denoted the section in which they worked. Bakers, waitresses and domestic staff were each issued with two 'Sister Dora' caps and drivers wore a peaked cap.

After a year, the women received a second uniform issue (other than the greatcoat). They were permitted to purchase civilian waterproofs.

There was an initial request that belts were not to be worn with their waterproofs but this was repealed due to comments made in some quarters that they resembled maternity clothes.

Not everything was officially issued and recruits were required to provide their own underclothes, nightclothes and toiletries, as well as a suitcase. For some of the women this proved to be difficult. Gwynne-Vaughan noted with regard to underclothes that 'while these were often excellent and usually neat and appropriate, instances occurred when they were in rags or hardly existed at all.'[20]

Many of the women were not keen on their uniform. Criticism was often levelled at the shoes, which were variously described as thick, stiff, clumsy, hard and like cast iron. Elizabeth Johnston complained that when she first wore hers she 'had great fun in the bedroom, practising "marking time" … . I got out of step; they were so heavy I could hardly lift them, and lost three steps out of twelve.'[21] The brown collars were unpopular and many workers purchased white or light coloured collars. The difficulty was that white collars were only for forewomen. This did not deter Ruby Ord:

> we bought light ones which we weren't allowed to wear but which we continued to wear. This is one of the things one learns early in life – if enough of you do something there's nothing that can be done about it. So it was a question of esprit de corps … our Corps not theirs and enough of us wore [them] that eventually they ignored them.[22]

The length of the coat frock was also problematic. In 1915, the hemline of civilian women's dresses was raised by several inches with the design of the 'war crinoline,' although this began to go out of fashion in 1916. The WAAC hemline in France was nine and a half inches from the ground and in the UK it was eight inches.[23] Many of the women in the Corps, however, considered this too be too long, particularly when undertaking physical work in the often muddy conditions in France. Ruby Ord commented that:

And of course when we arrived in France it seemed to rain all the time. And the roads were liquid mud and trailing skirts in the mud, we asked if we could be allowed to turn up the dresses and we were told that they must be nine inches from the ground. A big notice was put up in the camp and we changed that to nine inches from the waist … . We decided amongst ourselves, the rebels – after all, we were suffragettes, a number of us – and we said "Well we're going to cut them off at the length we want so that they can't make us let the hems down." So we just cut them off at the length we wanted and bound them round so that there was no question of letting them down. It was quite a respectable length, believe me, but not to their way of thinking. But you can see, as you walked the mud splashed up and we had only one dress. So if it was filthy dirty, you had to wear a filthy dirty dress.[24]

Gwynne-Vaughan considered at the time that the skirts were daringly short. However, in a letter to her former colleague Blanche Ireland, on the publication of her autobiography over twenty years later, she stated '[h]ow quaint the long skirts seem now …'[25]

Ruby Ord and her compatriots were not the only ones to alter their uniform. General Instructions No 1 for the WAAC in France, issued on 1 June 1917, stated that uniform 'will not be modified or added to. The badges of the Corps (but no other badges or ornaments) will be worn when in uniform.'[26] Some women, however, added adornments such as flowers and brooches or wore silk stockings but this resulted in punishment. This could be viewed as either the Army wanting to suppress their femininity, or as the military requirement for uniformity and the suppression of individuality.

The Assistant Controller of GHQ 1st Echelon recorded that she had to purchase extra material to strengthen some pairs of overalls as they shrank when washed.[27] The women were permitted to buy additional clothing, for example hats and shoes, if there was an official supply shortage and the fact that they did this from unofficial sources resulted in difficulties in maintaining consistency. This, as well as their own amendments, means that it can occasionally prove difficult to identify Corps officials and members by their uniform in contemporary photographs.

A number had their hair cut short or bobbed for hygienic reasons. Emily Rumbold, who worked as a storekeeper at Calais Docks, had her hair cut by a French male hairdresser in the town: '[w]e had to wait in turn with the men ... . Bobbed hair was most attractive really. ... [Had it short] for cleanliness, some of the girls' heads were not clean ... . My mother was horrified when I arrived home on leave.'[28]

Society's Initial View of the WAAC

Before the formation of the WAAC, much of society held a negative view of the women in military-style uniform joining voluntary organisations run primarily by and for the upper-middle and upper classes. They were accused of aping men and criticised for daring to wear the same khaki uniform as the male soldiers who fought and died for their country.

The announcement of the formation of the WAAC was accompanied by positive articles in national and local newspapers. This response was based on the fact that they acknowledged that there was a manpower shortage and not only was the employment of women with the Army part of the solution, it was sanctioned by the authorities. Further, it reflects the propaganda role fulfilled by newspapers at the time. The articles were careful not to portray the women as equal to soldiers but emphasised the auxiliary role which meant that men could be freed up to carry out what was considered to be more important work.

In March 1918, Fryniwyd Jesse considered that there had been a change in the way that society viewed women in uniform as a result of the establishment of the WAAC. She wrote that '[t]he thing was no longer a game at which women were making silly asses of themselves and pretending to be men; it had become regular, ordered, disciplined and worthy of respect. In short, uniform was no longer fancy dress.'[29]

Her view, and those expressed in the newspapers were not reflected in public opinion. Many women who joined the WAAC reported experiencing hostility from civilians at home, including verbal abuse and the drawing away of skirts as they passed. There are four key reasons that underpinned this behaviour.

First, there were concerns that the women would upset the order of society by challenging traditional gender roles. During the First World War, British women moved from the private to the public sphere in unprecedented numbers. Prior to the formation of the WAAC they took on jobs vacated by men (substitution) and worked in war industries. The potential impact on men returning from the war, for example on their pay, was problematic, but women in these roles were seen as necessary for the war effort. There was an expectation that traditional roles would resume once the war was over. The difficulty came when women were seen to be equal to men, and therefore a woman joining the Army and going overseas was considered a step too far. There was a belief held by some that women would become fighting soldiers and that this was not a role for a woman. They were even criticised in some quarters for smoking as this was considered the preserve of men. In a newspaper article that appealed for donations to a Young Women's Christian Association (YWCA) hut, the YWCA representative referred to the:

"silly habit" of smoking among members of the women's army … said they were going to make a strong appeal to all women to stop smoking, because they were taking something from the men – something that belonged to the men and not to women.[30]

At the same time, thousands of men were invalided home with physical and mental illnesses, which complicated the notion of the masculine soldier. It was also the first war in which men could apply to be registered as conscientious objectors.

Femininity was used as a propaganda tool to recruit men. The illustration of two women and a child on a recruitment poster stating

'Women of Britain say – "Go!"'[31] portrayed women as being in need of protection. Men were encouraged to fight for the women and children at home. In their book on the history of the WAAC published during the war, Edith Barton and Marguerite Cody wrote at the beginning of 1918 of the British woman that:

> must be fought for and protected in these modern days with even more chivalry, strength, and valour than in the long ago days of mediaeval ages. "It would be an awful war indeed if women came into the firing line," said one young soldier recently.[32]

If women left the relative safety of the UK and followed the men to France, the question could be asked – what were the men fighting for? This resulted in a paradox whereby a woman was expected to remain at home as a symbol of civilisation and all that was worth fighting for, as well as go to work in industry. In addition, their role as mothers was emphasised and the move of women into the public sphere was seen as a potential threat to the health of the nation.

Second, there was unease from some quarters that the women were being overtly masculine, not only by joining the male preserve of the Army but also by wearing a military uniform. This in turn was fed by a fear of feminism, manifested by the pre-war campaign for suffrage. There was a further fear associated with lesbianism. The First World War offered an opportunity to re-evaluate gender roles and sexual orientation, but it remained a taboo subject. It was not until the 1920s that lesbianism began to form part of a public discourse. Even then, the novel *The Well of Loneliness*[33] by Radclyffe Hall, which portrayed a lesbian ambulance driver behind the front line, was banned from publication in the UK in 1928.

Third, there was a widely held belief that women with questionable morals were enrolling with the WAAC with the sole intention of mixing with the men in France. This is explored in greater detail in Chapter 5.

Finally, the WAAC was aimed primarily at working class women and during the war this group was viewed with increasing suspicion and dislike by some in the middle classes. They were gaining greater independence as they moved into men's jobs and their wages were increasing. Concerns were raised about their new lifestyles, which were described in contrast to the life of the men in the trenches who were fighting to protect those very same women. This was particularly the case for the munitions workers who were often depicted as immoral, drunk and spending their money on luxury goods. This led to questions about the real motivation for women wanting to join the Army i.e. that it was not for patriotic reasons, but for independence and money.

During October and November 1917, in response to society's ongoing negative view of the Corps and as part of a recruitment drive, female journalists were deployed by the War Office to the WAAC camps in France. The War Diary for the WAAC attached to the Director General Transport and General Headquarters Club Units recorded that Gwynne-Vaughan inspected the women accompanied by five female press representatives: Grace Curnock (*Morning Post*); Mrs Lethbridge (unknown but may have been from the Army Intelligence Dept.); Miss Kennedy (*The Times* and *Daily Graphic*); Mary Frances Billington (*Daily Telegraph*); and Marguerite Cody (Press Association).[34] The visits resulted in further very positive reports in the newspapers at home. There was an emphasis on the feminine nature of their work i.e. traditionally female roles. Maguerite Cody wrote that '[d]ilution of the British Army began, as was most properly fitting, in the kitchen and messroom'[35] and that 'hundreds of women clerks … have released men for more manly and laborious tasks than typing or keeping ledgers.'[36] They described a picture of WAAC life in France as homely, including a description of '[t]he show bedroom in the hostel [which] had rose pink casement curtains with a lamp shade and cushions to match, and flowers and photographs made the picture complete.'[37] The articles were full of praise from the male officers with whom the women worked and the way in which the women had been accepted by the soldiers. The aim was to encourage recruitment and to reassure the families of women who were either considering enrolling or who were already in France. Indeed, this was the approach taken by the press throughout the war. Madame Tizoc, a French journalist working for *Le Petit Parisien*, also visited WAAC camps at this time. A translated version of her subsequent article was published in British newspapers in January 1918. It praised the WAAC, particularly the organisation and discipline, and questioned whether it was too late for the French to follow suit.

Reasons for Joining

Given that society had a negative view of the WAAC, why did women want to join? When examining primary sources, the answer is dependent on the individual, who is asking the question and when they are asking it. For example, journalists at the time may have selected quotes from women who cited patriotism as their motivation as it would support their propaganda-based articles. When interviewed in their latter years, some may have stated patriotism because they felt that was the answer they should give. Equally, it may well have been the genuine reason for their enrolment. Indeed, patriotism is the reason most often given by the women. Ruby Ord stated that:

> When the war came … we were fantastically patriotic. It was all patriotism. Not emotional in any other sense except for the sake of the country, it must be saved at all costs. What we stood for, everything we believed in, was threatened.[38]

Patriotism had different meanings for different women. For some, it meant being inspired by male friends and relatives who were willing to sacrifice their lives for their country and wanting to do the same. For others, it was the opportunity to release men to fight or to be directly involved in the war.

A number of academics and writers state that working class women joined the WAAC for the wages. Pay is not given as a reason by women in primary sources but it may be the case that they did not want to admit it. The majority of the women who enrolled were already engaged in paid war work and the WAAC did not offer the highest wages. The fact the WAAC offered paid work, however, did mean that working class women could join a uniformed service. Up until this time, organisations such as the FANY and WVR were voluntary and required women to pay for their own uniform. The Women's Legion had been the only uniformed service to provide paid work. Ironically, as the war progressed it was the middle class women who had initially been able to afford to carry out voluntary work who required a wage.

In addition to patriotism, the women cited a variety of reasons for enrolment. These can be viewed in terms of pull and push factors. The pull factors included a desire for adventure, a sense of belonging, freedom and independence. Annie Martin, a civil servant who enrolled as a telegraphist stated, when interviewed nearly sixty years later, '[p]erhaps I should put patriotism first of all but I've always had a wanderlust, I've always liked getting about. I joined up with a friend and we were fairly young. It was something new.'[39] Mabel Dymond Peel, who worked in Army Intelligence, wrote in her autobiography that '[t]here were certainly some members of the corps who were attracted by the novelty of the life and its excitements, and who were frankly out to enjoy themselves, but they were in the minority.'[40]

The push factors included: escaping the constraints of living at home; coping with, or seeking revenge for, the loss of a male relative; or getting away from harsh working conditions. The latter mainly concerned domestic workers, who carried out the same type of work in the WAAC but preferred the military environment of the camps in France to the private homes of their previous employers. Annie Martin also referred to push factors:

Conditions at the office were so difficult and so hard and life in England wasn't too easy then because of course by that time the air raids had started in London. So I had a number of reasons really why I joined up.[41]

The women received varying levels of support and opposition from their families. Amy Hall, who had been a hospital worker before enrolling in the Corps, described her family's reaction in the context of her brother's service:

> my poor dear parents were terribly upset. I was very, very thoughtless because my brother who was only four years older than me, he'd been in the Gallipoli landings … . It took him six months to be put right … . They let him come home for three weeks … and after reporting back to his unit they were sent to the Somme and he was killed … . So after saying I'd go abroad it was very cruel to my people.[42]

Ruby Ord, when asked about the reaction of her family, replied that 'I think they wished they had the courage to do the same … my family encouraged me, they didn't mind.'[43] Elsie Cooper also described the supportive reaction of a parent: 'I don't think they objected because mother always said that as a child she wanted to get away from where she was and she never had been able to, so she would not stop any of us.'[44]

Married women were allowed to apply and did not require their husband's approval. However, if her husband was in France, she could not serve there but was required to be based in the UK. There were concerns that married couples may regularly try and see each other and that this would have a negative effect on their work. It could be interpreted that the work of the man was considered to be of greater importance. However, as the woman was not able to fight, it was likely that of the two the woman would return, albeit in the WAAC, to the UK. As the numbers of fighting men decreased, a husband who was in a non-combative role may have been required to move up the line if deemed fit. A WAAC engaged to a man serving in France could remain in that country until they were married. Presumably it was believed that they were unlikely to want to see each other as regularly as a married couple. In a similar way to male volunteers, women often enrolled in the WAAC with their sisters or friends. An official arrangement was put in place to ensure that, where possible and if requested, friends and relatives were posted together.[45]

Ongoing Recruitment

As stated previously, the WAAC was oversubscribed in March 1917 but recruitment slowed in the following months to September 1917.

There were difficulties in the early recruitment of officials whereby Chalmers Watson wanted them to have had experience of regular work. This meant that the most suitable women were already engaged in war work. Officials were recruited directly by the War Office rather than through the Department of National Service.

Why were there also difficulties in recruiting women as members in the first few months? The concerns raised in April 1917 by the Department of National Service[46] regarding the recruitment pipeline have already been mentioned. On 26 June 1917, a conference was held between the War Office and the National Service Department at which a number of the causes were noted. These were set out in more detail in an internal memo drafted the following day by the National Service Department.[47] They included a lack of formal communication pathways between the departments resulting in confusion and friction, as well as no formal instructions being issued to Selection Boards and shared between departments. The National Service Department criticised the War Office for not providing them with returns detailing accepted candidates, which meant it was difficult to track progress against targets. It also complained that the War Office did not maintain reserve lists, which impacted on the flow of recruitment and resulted in the withdrawal of many women.

There appears to have been initial confusion regarding the restriction of married women working overseas at the same time as their husbands. ACI 537 published in March 1917 stated that no woman was eligible whose husband was serving overseas. The National Service Department reported that no such women had been put forward for selection, when actually the restriction was only when the man was serving in France. The memo also referred to an issue with references. A number of Selection Boards insisted that referees should be of significant social standing and refused many as not being good enough. This had implications for many of the working class women who did not necessarily know anyone engaged in a profession on the War Office approved list. Selection Boards had also refused applications where the referee had declined to confirm the nationality of both the applicant and her parents.

The National Service Department questioned the nationality restrictions. They noted that they could only interview women whose parents were British. It was recommended that this be relaxed as women had non-British fathers who nevertheless served in the British Army. They also recommended that women who passed the Selection Board but required spectacles or dentistry should receive treatment.

Finally, the National Service Department referred to pay as a barrier to recruitment, particularly of clerks. Prior to the conference, May Tennant (National Service Department) had made enquiries into the matter. She received reports that, due to low pay for clerks, a very high percentage of women had not progressed their applications or had withdrawn during the selection stages. This was exacerbated for some by the fact that they had dependents and needed security of work beyond the war.[48] One report set out the pay that thirteen applicants to one Selection Board were in receipt of and in most cases it was equal to, or above, the maximum scale in the WAAC. As a result, a number withdrew and others would only accept a higher grade clerkship. May Tennant also received evidence that a number who had qualified for the higher pay scale had agreed to take a lower rate because they did not want to lose the opportunity of getting out to France. This highlights the fact that the reasons why women joined were more complex than simply pay. The majority of clerks who signed up during these months were willing to enrol for a lower rate of pay due to patriotic reasons. However, the National Service Department expressed concerns that this source of women was becoming exhausted. This was quickly addressed and the rate of pay for clerks was increased. For example, a shorthand typist in France initially earned 28/- to 32/- per week but this was increased in July 1917 to 37/6 per week.[49]

There were further difficulties in recruiting telegraphists and telephonists through the General Post Office. Initially, free travelling passes were not made available and the women were expected to pay for their own travel if they wished to return to the UK during leave. In addition, the conditions of service stated that the women would serve for one year and be renewed by mutual consent at the end of that period. However, ACI 537 and the WAAC enrolment form stated one year or for the duration of the war, whichever was the longest. Unfortunately, in April 1917 the Postmaster General had stated in the House of Commons that the conditions originally stated were definite. This resulted in uncertainty among the women and a consequent lack of volunteers. The Postmaster General, concerned that others may withdraw their application, requested that the War Office allow the telegraphists and telephonists to enrol for one year.[50] The latter request was refused by the War Office as they did not want differing conditions of service within the Corps and did not believe that enrolling for the duration was a deterrent.

To increase recruitment in the summer of 1917, women who worked in government or essential occupations who had initially been asked not to apply, were now encouraged to seek their employers' permission. The employers were asked to consider the balance between inconvenience and the need to substitute men in France. The Department of National Service had been pushing for this approach since the beginning of April 1917.

In addition to advertising for recruits, the National Service Department directly approached employers in specific work areas. In July 1917, for example, they interviewed the managing director of a bakery who agreed to put up WAAC recruitment notices in his bakehouses.[51]

There was a significant difference between the number of applications and the number finally enrolled. For example, between 21 March 1917 and 29 June 1917 there were 8,017 applications for clerical posts, of which 4,309 were summoned to sixty-six Boards (including thirty in London) of which 2,207 were finally enrolled.[52]

By the middle of July 1917, approximately 1,000 WAACs had been sent to France. By the end of August 1917 there were 2,000 WAACs in France and the number was increasing by fifty per week.[53]

On 16 July 1917, after publication of ACI 1069, a conference was held by Lord Derby at the War Office and attended by the National Service Department and the Employment Department. Lord Derby questioned whether recruitment to the WAAC should continue to be carried out by the National Service Department. Arrangements were subsequently made to transfer recruitment to Frances Durham at the Employment Department of the Ministry of Labour. A number of staff transferred with the work, but at the beginning of August 1917, May Tennant and Violet Markham resigned from the Women's Section of the National Service Department as a direct result of the decision. The recruiting process was improved as women could apply directly at their local Employment Exchange. However, this could have had a negative impact on women from the middle classes who, according to the press, felt uncomfortable visiting their local Exchange. There were nine local recruiting areas with a female recruiting controller. Women were given assistance in arranging their travel to the Selection Boards. The Boards were required to process 400 women a week. There was a local hostel to which women were sent before going to their unit. These changes partly account for the increase in recruitment in September 1917.

There was also an increase at this time due to the extension of recruitment to Ireland. In May 1917, the National Service Department had requested that the War Office consider holding a Selection Board in Ireland.[54] They had been made aware by the equivalent Irish department that there were many women who wanted to apply. The War Office wanted to wait as a new recruitment process for Ireland was under consideration and ACI 1069 had not been published. In July 1917, the National Service Department made further strong representation to the War Office who granted approval by the end of the month. A Selection Board and Hostel were subsequently established in Dublin.

By September 1917, all 6,000 of the Women's Legion Cookery Section staff had been transferred to the WAAC.[55] They wore the WAAC uniform but were allowed to wear their Women's Legion badge on their collars. There remained, however, a shortage of domestic staff. In September 1917, recruitment pamphlets and articles in national newspapers stated that the War Office needed 10,000 women by the end of October 1917 and 40,000 before Christmas 1917 (for service both at home and overseas). A number of the articles took the form of letters home supposedly from WAACs, written in a conversational style and encouraging women at home to enrol. This campaign was another factor in the increase in recruitment during this month. AG11 undertook to hold forty-two Selection Boards per week to deal with the high number of applicants.[56] However, the increase in applications was short-lived.

On 9 October 1917, Sir Auckland Geddes (Director of National Service),[57] made a speech in Nottingham in which he called for women to volunteer to join the WAAC. In terms of domestic workers, he stated that:

> we want to avoid drawing away the single-handed maids of the small middle class homes which the mother with several young children can hardly manage alone without some help. We want to draw the women with experience of domestic work from the larger households in which more than three servants in all are kept.[58]

Many of the young women domestics were attracted to the high wages of the munitions factories. The older women domestics had established themselves in good positions to which they may not have been easily able to return and were incomparable to the employment being offered by the WAAC.

A determined recruitment campaign began in November 1917. A recruitment hut, set up in London's Trafalgar Square, was opened at a ceremony with George Henry Roberts (Minister for Labour) and Sir Nevil Macready. Sir Auckland Geddes called not only for domestics but also for middle class women to leave non-essential war work and join the WAAC. The press once again asked women to enrol and reported on local recruitment drives, attended by WAAC representatives, key female members of local communities, councillors and Employment Exchange staff. Religious leaders also attended many of the meetings. Indeed, the Bishop of Birmingham was reported to state at a recruitment meeting in the city that:

> The clergy ... could do much for the movement, and ... they might well call attention to the needs of the Army from the pulpits and elsewhere. ... The movement [was] one calculated to be of great use in the days of peace, as it would strengthen and discipline the character of the women.[59]

Recruitment continued throughout the war through cinema, the press, public meetings and even women sitting at tables outside London department stores. Posters declared 'Women Urgently Wanted for the WAAC' and provided details on the categories of work available that would free men up for the Front. An example can be found at plate one. The Women's War Services Exhibition was opened at Harrods on 11 February 1918 and ran for two weeks. The exhibition, organised by the Ministry of Labour, was opened by Princess Arthur of Connaught. The aim was to encourage women to apply for enrolment by portraying life and work in the Women's Services and Women's Land Army using photographs and lectures, as well as displays and uniforms. The exhibition proved to be very popular and opening times were extended. Queen Mary attended on the final day and met women who worked in the Women's Services, including the WAAC.

Women from Ireland were enrolled, as well as from further afield, for example the Commonwealth countries of South Africa, Canada and New Zealand. Thirty-five women from Australia joined the Corps, including Dr Phoebe Chapple of the RAMC attached to the WAAC.

At the beginning of 1918, the problem of recruiting officials continued. As previously stated, the senior women of the WAAC wanted young ladies from the upper-middle classes to command the lower grades. Further, they preferred them to be married and engaged in a profession.

Although roles and responsibilities of government departments regarding recruitment had been agreed in 1917, there were subsequent issues. In January 1918, the Ministry of National Service proposed that it take forward recruitment of women to the three Women's Services. This was partly driven by a concern that not all women were content to apply through Employment Exchanges as they were considered to be for the working classes. George Roberts was not impressed and wrote to Sir Auckland Geddes, making it clear that recruitment was his responsibility and was critical of the way in which the Ministry of National Service officials had gone about the matter. In his view the Ministry of National Service was responsible for policy and prioritisation. Sir Auckland Geddes replied that he had been so busy as to not be acquainted with the detail and had told his officials to 'hold their horses.'[60] George Roberts was supported by the War Office, the Air Council, the Admiralty and the Treasury. In March 1918, both ministries and the three Women's Services agreed to joint Selection and Medical Boards for the WAAC, WRNS and Women's Royal Air Force (WRAF), as well as shared receiving depot hostels.

The number of new recruits reached its height between March and May 1918 and remained high through the summer in comparison with the same period in 1917. By this stage, the need for women to substitute men in industry at home had stabilised and munitions factories were making women redundant. The requirement for women overseas was still increasing. In June 1918, 2,939 women were needed in France and the main requirement was for cooks, general domestics and store women, as well as fitters and machinists.[61]

Gwynne-Vaughan stated that by the end of the war, 56,000 women had served in the WAAC[62] and the number 57,000 is often referred to in secondary sources. Ten thousand women served in the Corps in France.[63]

Chapter 3

Daily Life

Travel to France

On 31 March 1917, the first draft of women left England for France. Unit Administrator May Finlay and her fourteen cooks and waitresses had been the first to transfer from the Women's Legion.[1] They were to staff the Expeditionary Force Canteen (EFC) Officers Club in Abbeville. They encountered a minor setback when May Finlay contracted measles within ten days and their accommodation had to be disinfected. On 4 April 1917, the second draft of twenty-seven women led by Deputy Unit Administrator M.W. Atkinson arrived in France to staff the EFC Officers Club in Boulogne.[2]

On 7 April 1917, the third draft of twenty-two women clerks disembarked at Boulogne and was bound for the Directorate of Forestry in Le Touquet. This draft, led by Deputy Unit Administrator E.F. Grundy, included women who had not transferred from the Women's Legion. They did not have a comfortable journey because, although they reached their camp on the same day, they had to spend a few hours at Boulogne and did not have sufficient rations. This led Gwynne-Vaughan to later establish a hostel at the port to facilitate the movement of women between dockside and camp. When the third draft of women arrived at their camp, they found that the local hospitals were in need of beds. In response, they gave up their bedsteads without any fuss and volunteered to sleep under the same conditions as the men they were replacing.[3]

These drafts and those that were to follow them over the next eighteen months travelled to Boulogne. However, some drafts did sail to Le Havre. The sea voyage was hazardous. The women donned life belts and their boats were escorted through mined waters by naval destroyers that endeavoured to protect them from enemy submarines. A WAAC chief controller, based in the UK, died in these perilous waters. Violet Long, the sister of Florence Leach, drowned in August 1918 on a return journey from France when the hospital ship *Warilda* was torpedoed. Violet Long's orderly, Charlotte Trowell, survived and described what happened after she had reached the relative safety of a lifeboat:

> I shall never forget the end of Mrs Long. She clung to the boat into which I had been dragged, and I caught hold of her by the hair. She exclaimed, "Oh, save me, my feet are fastened, I have lost a foot!" Her feet had become entangled in some rope. Strenuous efforts succeeded in freeing her limbs, and a Southampton sailor tried hard to get her into the boat, but she collapsed suddenly, fell back, and was drowned.[4]

Violet Long left behind a husband and two little girls. The danger at sea was further demonstrated by the death of an assistant administrator, May Westwell, who was drowned on 10 October 1918 when RMS *Leinster* was torpedoed in the Irish Sea on its way to Holyhead from Dublin.

Charlotte Bottomley enrolled as a store woman and later transferred to telephony, which had been her civilian job. After the excitement of learning that she was in a draft to go overseas, she described her subsequent voyage in somewhat negative terms:

> We embarked at 0545 on to a troop ship. This is the point at which I realised that there was a war on. Some of the men on board were extremely rude to us, some dully resented our intrusion, others regarded us as a joke. … We'd been told before that we should have this sort of thing to contend with and to maintain our dignity in all cases. At 1830 the ship began to move and I shall never forget

the awful feeling I had as I saw my beloved country slipping away from view.[5]

Once they reached Boulogne, they were met on the quayside by the WAAC draft receiving officer. She provided instructions to the official travelling with the draft and organised the collection of their luggage. Many of the women stayed overnight at the famous 'Boathouse', which was, in fact, a boating club headquarters on the River Liane. The accommodation was run by a forewoman and a worker, who came in from their own quarters to prepare the accommodation for each draft. The drafts of women slept on the floor on palliasses or 'biscuits' filled with straw, which formed a mattress. Meanwhile, the administrator slept on a bed on a raised platform. The lamps were often kept on during the night to discourage rats. Dorothy Pickford, an assistant administrator and later unit administrator, wrote home of her draft that:

> The girls were very good tho' awfully excited, I only had to call for silence twice, but I sounded exceedingly severe. Before turning in, I dressed and bandaged half a dozen vaccination arms, all as if I had done it all my life.[6]

Charlotte Bottomley described how her journey did not improve on reaching Boulogne:

> We had a very disturbed night as there were troops coming down from the line all night, whistling and singing and shouting on their way up the hill to the delousing station. Incidentally, the blankets which we slept in had not been disinfected after being previously used by troops. Consequently several of us developed body lice which wasn't a nice way to start our active service.[7]

Annie Martin described it as 'a shocking affair. Some of the girls said that rats ran over their faces and you could see the river through the boards.'[8]

In the morning, the women were taken to the train station or collected by army truck for onward transport to their final destination. Elizabeth Johnston wrote in her diary of the train journey from Boulogne to Calais:

> At intervals, fairly frequent, it stopped, miles from anywhere. At such times a few Tommies got out and had a snowball fight ... . I enjoyed it thoroughly. We had rations with us, so had a jolly little picnic during this quaint journey. On reaching [our] destination our Tommy co-travellers insisted on carrying our luggage, in spite of the fact that they had enough to do looking after their own kit.[9]

Her journey, however, finished with her marching ankle deep in melted snow and mud to the camp.

WAAC Camps

The WAAC headquarters was located in a house in Abbeville from 1 June 1917 to 13 June 1918 when it moved to a villa in St Valery-sur-Somme, a nearby town but in the same area. By 1919, it had moved to Wimereux.

The WAAC was based in eight areas from north to south as follows: Calais, Boulogne, St Omer, Étaples, Abbeville, Dieppe, Le Havre and Rouen. Those attached to the American Expeditionary Force (AEF) were based in Bourges, as well as Tours to the south of Paris. For each of these areas there was an area controller and these women were responsible for accommodation, rations and discipline, as well as overseeing the work within the camps. Base depots were located in Étaples and Le Havre, which were used to accommodate drafts when they first arrived in France and also women who were transferring between areas.

In most cases, an area had a camp or camps (variously named Queen Mary Camp, Queen Alexandra Camp or Camp 1, 2, etc.) but also a variety of accommodation types in nearby towns and villages. For example, Étaples had a camp in the town but the women also lived in nearby Le Touquet in cottages by the sea. Gwynne-Vaughan had identified these properties as having the potential to house women when she first visited in February 1917. WAACs also lived in hotels and old houses, collectively referred to as hostels. Elizabeth Johnston briefly lived and worked in the Archbishop's Palace in Rouen and appreciated the stark difference to camp life:

> this is heaven. Our bedroom, where eight are accommodated, used to be the Dining Hall. The walls are panelled … . Above the marble and beautifully carved fireplace, there is a large mirror, reaching to the ceiling … . Camellias are in bloom … . In one corner there is a piano … . We usually go to sleep to the strains of sweet music.[10]

Each camp or hostel was run by a unit administrator and deputy administrator. The number of officials was dependent on the size of the camp. The responsibilities of the administrator and her staff included day-to-day running of the camp or hostel, discipline and overseeing the women's entertainments. The housework was carried out by WAAC members in the Household Section.

The first camp was opened in the middle of May 1917 and others quickly followed. The WAAC War Diaries provide an insight into how the camps were established and their subsequent growth. For example, on 5 August 1917, Mary Sophia Frood took over duties as area controller of Abbeville after being promoted from unit administrator at the Advanced Mechanical Transport Depot (AMTD) in Abbeville. On day one she arranged for a fatigue party to clean and furnish the headquarters at 122, Rue St Gilles. By 1 September 1917, Abbeville had Camp 1 at Mautort, Camp 2 on the Boulogne Road (which opened on 21 August 1917), a draft of WAACs had been sent to the Fourth Army Infantry School in Flixecourt and an inspection at the Third Army School in Auxi-le-Château had taken place to review accommodation for thirty cooks. In total, there were fifteen officials and 288 members.

Camp 3 on the Amiens Road was opened on 23 September 1917. By 31 January 1918 there were nineteen officials, 644 members and two doctors.[11]

The camps were normally situated outside of the main town and away from the men's camps. The WAACs were housed either in wooden huts, which held between ten to thirty women or Nissen huts, which held eight to twelve women. The signallers slept separately to the others, often in the smaller Nissen huts, as they worked day and night shifts. The Nissen huts contained a stove, as well as a separate cubicle for the forewoman or assistant forewoman. The windows were often covered with oiled canvas rather than glass.

Sleeping arrangements were rather basic. Each bed had three straw filled biscuits, one pillow and two blankets but no sheets or pillow cases. Each morning, all had to be folded and left at the end of the bed for inspection.

The women did personalise their accommodation where possible with the addition of curtains, photographs, flowers and pictures. Fryniwyd Jesse described the importance of such decoration within the otherwise basic and functional army accommodation: '[y]ou will always see in every cubicle, above every bed in a long hut, the girl's own private gallery, the *lares and penates* which make of her, in her bed at least, an individual.'[12] Plate two shows a watercolour painting by the artist Beatrice Lithiby. In *The Workers' Quarters, Queen Mary's Army Auxiliary Corps: Queen Elizabeth Camp, Vendroux*,[13] she painted vases of flowers, non-army issue blankets, pictures, photographs and a sign stating 'Smile Damn You Smile.' The image is of a homely scene, more reminiscent of a girl's bedroom than army quarters. This was one of the few areas in their military life in which they could express their femininity and individuality. The artist was a member of the Corps and further information about her can be found in Chapter 8.

The huts in which the officials slept were much the same as those for the workers. However, due to the fact that there were fewer of them in each hut, they had room for extra furniture. In some camps, the officials had their own dining room and sitting room, as well as an office.

Also on camp was a sick bay, administrator's hut, recreation room or hut, cook hut, mess hut and ablution block. The latter, which contained bath tubs, received hot water from boilers. Ruby Ord recalled that '[w]e had rotas for baths, tin baths … you were lucky if the water was hot on your night … . We were reasonably clean. That didn't worry me too much as long as we weren't lousy and none of us were.'[14]

The female journalists who visited the camps at the end of 1917 wrote of the comfort and homeliness to be found in the women's camps. They referred to electric light, spring beds and pillows, flowerbeds and green strips of lawn. Although not untrue, it was an idealistic picture intended to encourage women to volunteer for enrolment.

Conditions could be challenging, for example there were rats to contend with and when it rained the ground quickly turned to mud so that duckboards needed to be laid down. The winter of 1917 was particularly severe and the women described frozen pipes and using melted snow for drinking and washing. Mabel Peel wrote of the harsh wintry conditions that:

> The sponge that one put down for a moment in the morning wash, froze instantly to its tin recipient, the towels hung stiff and hard ready to scrape our skin, and we frequently had to take the top blanket to the stove, not to air it, but to thaw it. We discovered that by putting brown paper between the spring mattress and the biscuits, we kept a little warmer and dryer, and most of us adopted this plan.[15]

The women, however, were aware that the conditions were incomparable to those experienced by men at the Front. Elizabeth Johnston wrote home that:

> Life in the Army isn't just a "Home from Home," as the popular advertisement has it, but we do not expect it to be, and are prepared

for hardships. The mud is terrible, and since it is so bad here, it helps us to realise how unspeakable are the conditions further up the line. ... However, no one grouses, soldiers don't, do they?[16]

Food

One element that the women did complain about, both at the time and in their recollections, was the food. Ruby Ord's description is representative of the majority:

When we arrived there were no rations for us to begin with so we had army biscuits and some cheese, I think. Eventually they got some bread which was green. The Australians had a bakery in Calais but we never had any fresh bread in spite of it. It was always stale. ... The rations were quite good but it was badly handled, badly cooked and nobody seemed to be worried.[17]

The questionable handling of the food is further illustrated by Charlotte Bottomley who recalled of the Machonichie stew that:

one time I found a soldier's button in it, a brass button and another time I found a tin disc which had come out of the Machonichie tin, another time I found the cupboard key in it. They weren't at all fussy.[18]

Out of the 14/- deducted from non-domestic staff, 10/- was allocated to food.[19] It was not permitted to spend more than 10/- per head. If this was not spent, the difference was added to the hostel fund and used to improve living conditions, for example buying a gramophone or flowers. It was made clear that, to maintain the women's health, expenditure on food was not to be reduced below what was necessary. The fund could also be drawn on if there was a deficit for the food bill in any week.

Their rations, which were slightly smaller than those given to the men in the lines of communication, consisted mainly of army biscuits, bread (a sixth to an eighth of a loaf), margarine, jam, cheese, rice and bully beef. They did receive food parcels from home but after a while they could not rely on them due to rationing, which was introduced in the UK in 1918. Instead, they supplemented their rations when possible from establishments outside of the camp, for example the canteens run by the Salvation Army, YWCA and the Young Men's Christian Association (YMCA). Cafés and restaurants were out of bounds, except for a few recognised tea shops. The canteens supplied them with tea, biscuits and chocolate. Elizabeth Johnston wrote home about the food provided at a WAAC club in Rouen, which was likely run by the YWCA:

> we can have home-baked scones and pancakes, and lovely tea with sugar and cow's milk in it. Also real butter on our scones and home-made apple jelly, and – fried potatoes! … Also, we can have fresh eggs, boiled or fried, at three-pence each.[20]

The purchase of extra food from these sources was dependent on supply and the women having sufficient funds. Green vegetables and fresh milk were in short supply and the women often purchased tins of condensed milk.

There is evidence of one WAAC unit that tried to be self-sufficient. In March 1918, GHQ 2nd Echelon purchased a pig and the Agricultural Office purchased half an acre of land near the camp for potatoes and other vegetables. A few days later, a WAAC working party prepared the ground for planting.[21] Allotments were common at the camps. Dorothy Pickford wrote home of a wonderful afternoon that she had spent:

> digging furiously for an hour and a half, aided by about six Tommies and four girls. They all worked together well with no nonsense, and the corporal in charge, who was too grand a man to dig himself, kept off the crowds of small French gamins.[22]

Medical Care

While they were overseas, the women ceased to be insurable and therefore not eligible for any benefits under the National Insurance Act. They did benefit from the organised provision of free medical care. During the first few months that the WAAC was in France, army medical officers dealt with any women who fell ill, albeit minor cases were often dealt with by ex-VADs who had joined the WAAC.

Chalmers Watson was all too well aware of what was required in terms of medical care as she was herself a doctor. She and Gwynne-Vaughan wanted female doctors working with the RAMC to be formed into a section with responsibility for the WAAC. This included running the Medical Boards in the UK which were part of the recruitment process, as well as being responsible for the health and well-being of the women in France. The War Office agreed to their proposals and the RAMC formed an Auxiliary Section which was responsible for the medical services of the WAAC under ACI 1676 on 12 November 1917. The section was staffed by women and came under control of the Director General, Army Medical Services. As in the WAAC, the female doctors had civilian status and therefore no formal rank.

In France, the most senior post was the Controller of Medical Services (Overseas) and was filled by Dr Laura Sandeman. She was 55 years of age and had run a medical practice in Aberdeen for many years. She had refused the post twice because the War Office Finance Department refused to pay her the salary of a man equivalent to her grade and instead they offered a little over half of the proposed £700 per year. Chalmers Watson, assisted by her brother Sir Auckland Geddes, pursued the matter with Lord Derby. The latter was not in favour but had little choice otherwise the post of Controller would not be filled. He eventually agreed to equal pay for Dr Laura Sandeman and she arrived for duty in Abbeville on 14 October 1917.[23] She wore RAMC badges and shoulder straps but the fleur-de-lis and two roses of a WAAC chief controller.

She was closely followed to France by Dr Phoebe Chapple, an Australian who had moved to the UK to join the RAMC after becoming frustrated by the fact that women doctors were not able to join the Australian Army. Charlotte Bottomley recalled that it was Dr Phoebe Chapple who diagnosed her appendicitis. She had concluded that it had been caused by Charlotte sucking on icicles found hanging from the mess hall roof when water was scarce.[24]

Dr Laura Sandeman was supported by assistant (area) medical controllers who were responsible for inspecting sites and buildings used by the WAAC for accommodation or employment, hospitals, rest camps and WAAC units. This also included the review of rations, clothing, exercise and working hours. They, in turn, were supported by female medical officials, who additionally held daily inspections of women who had reported sick. They all wore a similar uniform to the WAACs, including WAAC rank (or grade) badges on their shoulder straps but wore RAMC collar and hat badges.

In small establishments, one WAAC forewoman was to have had VAD or nursing experience if possible but in larger establishments such as camps, where there was a dedicated sick bay, there was a trained nurse appointed by the controller who was supported by a WAAC orderly.

If required, WAACs could be admitted to a military hospital. If there was a ward set aside in a military hospital for the WAAC, the medical official for that base would oversee the care of the women. The WAACs were usually placed in wards attached to military hospitals for nurses, known as Sick Sisters' Hospitals. When she was in France, Marguerite Cody visited a Sick Sister's Hospital in a thirteenth century chateau. She later wrote that:

> The WAAC ward when I visited it had only four patients in bed, suffering from nothing worse than colds and rheumatism ... . Their ward had been one of the sitting-rooms of the chateau, which has been let furnished. Crimson curtains framed the windows, while the gilt and white of the heavy chandeliers and the moulded plaster of the ceilings spoke of a different century.[25]

The photograph at plate two is of WAACs in a ward attached to the Sick Sisters' Hospital in Rouen. It shows a number of women confined to their beds in the sparsely furnished wooden hut, while others are well enough to be dressed and seated. The British Red Cross Society (BRCS) provided funds to the hospitals to pay for items that made the women's stay more comfortable, for example books and games.

On their discharge from the hospital, a decision was made as to whether they should rejoin their unit, return to the UK for permanent or temporary home service, return to hospital in the UK (for example the female-run military hospital in Endell Street, London) or be discharged from service. From April 1918, members of the WAAC were entitled to receive the Silver War Badge, awarded to those discharged on medical grounds.

The BRCS also established a number of convalescent homes that were shared by the WAACs and nurses. These were located in Hardelot, at the Villa de Rose in Étretat and at a villa in Le Touquet belonging to Lady Angela Forbes. Charlotte Bottomley stayed at the latter when recovering after her appendix operation and considered it to be just the place for a convalescent home.[26] A further convalescent home in Souverain-Moulin was for WAAC officials.

Dental treatment was provided for members but officials only received treatment if an army dentist was available.

The emphasis on health and fitness and the provision of high quality care resulted in a healthy corps of women. At the end of 1917, the Controller of Medical Services (Overseas) reported that the sickness rate amongst the WAAC was 1.6 per cent, compared to the 4 per cent expected amongst normally healthy people living together. In March 1918, a report by a Commission of Enquiry stated that:

The open air life whatever its disadvantages in cold and muddy weather has apparently many compensations and our general impression of the physical conditions of the girls was one of abounding good health. This impression was borne out by the official figures of sickness which are very low, namely, 2.5 per cent in hospital.[27]

The theme of outdoor life and the subsequent health benefits can be found throughout the primary sources, including photographs and oral testimony. Ruby Ord, when asked about the health of the Corps, replied 'I was certainly fit. I'd never been so well and I think most of the girls were. … And we had plenty of outdoors … everything was al fresco. The fresh air was coming in all the while, everywhere …'[28]

Recreation and Entertainment

To maintain morale and good health, the women were encouraged to relax during their time away from work. WAAC officials and workers, however, were not permitted to mix socially. Each camp or hostel had a recreation hut or room, supplemented by YWCA huts within camps or in the nearby towns. The first YWCA hut to open in France was in Abbeville. Run by YWCA staff, they often contained a library, letter writing tables, piano and sometimes provided food, as well as classes in French and English literature. Charlotte Bottomley referred to:

> two very noble ladies that looked after our YWCA. They were very, very kind. You know, when I think back, they were marvellous really. They got us all sorts of things from home that were difficult to come by such as sanitary pads … they went to great trouble to get things for us, birthday cards and stuff … that we couldn't get locally.[29]

The YWCA appealed to the people at home to fund huts for the WAAC, often taking out newspaper adverts.

The YWCA and Entertainments National Service Association (ENSA) organised concerts, including those put on by Lena Ashwell – an actress and theatre manager. Elizabeth Johnston attended one of her concerts in a YWCA hut in Rouen and wrote home that:

It was splendid; all London artistes; two male artistes, both wounded and discharged men. Lena Ashwell herself recited, and, oh, how splendidly she did it. You could have heard a pin fall – her audience sat tense, and waiting for each word. She is a most fascinating person.[30]

The WAACs themselves established concert parties and put on variety shows and amateur dramatic productions.

To promote mental and physical health, sport and team working were actively encouraged. The WAACs participated in hockey, cricket and tennis and often took part in events with the men. Elizabeth Johnston was a keen hockey player and described a particularly enjoyable game which took her mind briefly off of the war:

I was playing in a hockey match up at "Camps." … There are Indian and American and Australian camps; also British … . It is a lovely place! Signal girls were playing a team of Camp men; two of the men were Internationals – one had played for India. What a game it was! I was in prime form and played a good game, shooting a goal; and that is something when you've to take the ball through a forward line whose mainstay is an International.[31]

The women even took part in folk dancing. There were also excursions to seaside resorts, such as Le Touquet, where the women could bathe and take walks along the dunes.

The entertainment and sport contributed to the strong relationships built between the women who lived and worked in close quarters. Elizabeth Johnston wrote of the women with whom she shared a hut in a camp outside Rouen:

We are so happy in our hut. Everybody borrows and lends; we swop [sic] continually, the whole secret is "*bonne camaraderie.*" Whoever is in first makes the beds for the others and fills the hot water bags, then gets into her own bed and sits up waiting for the late workers.[32]

Army's View of the WAAC

How were the WAACs viewed by the men when they first went out to France? Gwynne-Vaughan encountered objections when she went out in March 1917 as the army officers were concerned about the impact that the women would have in the hitherto male environment of the Army. Gwynne-Vaughan wrote that the Army viewed them as an 'alien element.'[33] They were also aggrieved by the notion that women may hold similar or higher rank (or grade equivalent) to them. The situation was not improved by Gwynne-Vaughan's early emphasis on the WAAC as a military Corps. Back in London, Chalmers Watson received complaints about the militaristic nature of the WAAC in France.

The base camps where the women worked were transitory. Men from France, Belgium, Britain and the Commonwealth passed through on their way up to the line or back to hospitals or home. However, the WAACs did get to know the men who were based in the camps, particularly those that they worked with. The women initially experienced resentment from a number of the men. This was primarily because the men were being freed to move up the line and either did not want to go or considered that the women had little understanding of what conditions they would face in the trenches. Nora Barker, who enrolled as a gardener, recalled asking one of Gwynne-Vaughan's drivers one night why she was crying and received the answer that '"[y]ou know what the men up at the camp say? ... They say we've been brought out here to release men to their death."'[34] In addition, some were fearful that the Army, particularly the support roles in the lines of communication, would become emasculated. It was not only the men who expressed resentment, but also women who were already working behind the lines, for example nurses and canteen workers. Emily Rumbold referred to women running a canteen who said:

"We don't serve women here." They sent a complaint to our officers at the camp and said that they were not going to serve any English women at their canteens. So our officers were very furious about it. Of course we were rather furious because we had nowhere to get cups of tea or buy English soap ... and so our people took it up with headquarters ... and they had to allow us to go in again.[35]

The men gave the women a variety of nicknames including Waxworks, Brownies, Quacks, Polly Atkins and Chocolate Soldiers. It was not long, however, before the men grew accustomed to them. There may have been a number of reasons for this change. For example, once the men who could be freed up had moved up the line, the remaining men were those who would not be replaced due to their lower category of fitness or had roles not suitable for substitution by women. These men may have felt less antagonistic towards the WAACs. Equally, it may have been that the men became aware of the importance of the contribution that the women made, enjoyed their company and developed friendships. Ruby Ord, when questioned how she was treated by the male officers and men replied, '[n]ot very well when we first went out but they did adapt and they were very nice, they couldn't have been nicer ... the people we worked with, this is. ... [There was] very little strife. ... Generally speaking relationships were pleasant.'[36] Mabel Peel noted the men in her office were 'unfailingly polite and courteous to us women, and appreciated to the full any advance towards friendliness that we made to them.'[37] The attitude of the men was also observed in official quarters. A report commissioned by George Roberts in 1918 stated that:

Base Commandants and other officers ... have spoken to us in warm terms of the work of the WAAC. ... The appreciation shown by the soldiers for the work of the women and their obvious good will towards the Corps made a pleasant impression on the Commission. We were often told of the help and assistance given in the camps by soldiers of all ranks to individual Units which had resulted in greater amenities of life being provided for the girls.[38]

The Army initially had grave concerns about socialising between the men and the WAACs. Nurses and VADs were not allowed to mix with the men when off duty and the Army wanted to apply the same rule to the WAAC. In later years, Gwynne-Vaughan often quoted an officer who had stated at an early conference that they would have to wire all the woods on the lines of communication. She had replied that if that were to be the case, many couples would simply climb over. Gwynne-Vaughan was keen that mixing and socialising between the sexes be actively encouraged and she argued her position well. The Army eventually agreed with her that the men and women would meet and that it was better for discipline that this take place in sanctioned ways rather than covertly. Dorothy Pickford was well aware that the processes put in place were flouted, writing home that:

> I have just made an enemy for life by refusing a pass to a woman to go out with her "friend" alone. This is strictly against all rules, they may go for walks with their best boys but they must be two together. It seems rather an ostrich attitude, as of course they separate at the gate and only meet again when the pass has to be given up.[39]

Socialising, however, was not permitted between army officers and WAAC workers, including relatives, without special permission from a WAAC administrator. This was a principle with which both the Army and Gwynne-Vaughan were in agreement. The rule was often flouted by officers and workers, who met in private hotel rooms for meals. Elsie Cooper recalled being taken to Le Touquet by a Canadian officer:

> he had booked a private room which didn't suit me at all but I consider he was an officer ... I wasn't supposed to be seen out with an officer and I hadn't got a pass so it was alright. But after

that he deliberately delayed the return so that I would miss the roll call.[40]

She was caught returning to the depot but when she reported to her own officer she was told '[a]lright, child, run away and don't do it again'.[41]

As well as the mixed sporting events, for example hockey, tennis and cricket, WAAC workers were invited to concerts and dances got up by the men. In turn, the women were allowed to invite men to concerts, dances and other entertainments that they had arranged. Written permission was required from the WAAC administrator in the form of a pass issued to each man. The women were allowed to meet with men in places of amusement outside of the camps, for example YMCA huts. If this took place in the evening, they were required to obtain a pass, go as a group and be escorted by a forewoman. Elsie Cooper was surprised that the men and women could mix and remembered a speech given to her draft by the official on their arrival in Étaples in which they were told 'that we could make friends with the boys. We were to be very careful because there were plenty to choose from, we were to choose the right ones.'[42]

In September 1917, the Area Controller for GHQ 1st Echelon recorded in the War Diary that, in routine orders, Gwynne-Vaughan had banned all mixed theatricals,[43] i.e. concert parties made up of men and women. It had caused great distress and she believed it would be almost impossible to find alternative entertainment for the women during the long winter evenings. In spite of the order, they held a general meeting the following month and elected a mixed Amusements Committee.

The socialising between the WAACs and the men contributed to the successful development of the Corps. They were able to build a strong relationship with the men they worked with which fostered a spirit of co-operation. The men appreciated the environment that the women were able to provide them with when they were resting behind the lines. One soldier wrote a letter to his local newspaper at home in which he described a WAAC concert to which his regiment had been invited. He observed that:

> Here all war was forgotten. From time to time the room would echo to merry laughter. … It was a happy evening and tonight … there is many a sentry on his post, as he watches and waits for the enemy, who blesses those few hours respite from the war.[44]

Contrary to the view expressed by some on the establishment of the WAAC, it may well have been that these very occasions shared by men and women behind the line were a reminder to the men of what they were fighting for.

Marriages did occur and required permission from both the woman's chief controller and the man's commanding officer. Discretion was shown by allowing them to spend a week in a 'Honeymoon Cottage' with the permission of the Commander in Chief. The woman was then required to return to the UK if her husband was serving in France, as it was not permitted for a WAAC to serve in the same theatre of war as her husband.

The WAACs not only lived alongside soldiers of the Commonwealth but also German POWs and the Chinese Labour Corps. In general, the WAACs got on well with the German POWs. Ruby Ord stated that '[w]e had to moderate the views we had when we left England about them because they were boys like one's own brothers.'[45] The WAACs didn't mix with the prisoners but Ruby Ord recalled that they prepared hut floors for them for dances and that:

> Some of them were awfully nice fellows, these German prisoners. We weren't allowed to fraternise with them, if we were seen speaking to them we'd helped to lose the war. But they were nice and they were victims of the situation the same as we were. And they did all sorts of things for us, I mean if people in camp had known they'd have been horrified. … [They] cut up wood etc. to

enable us to have illegal fires … . They deposited [the wood] in caches we knew about.[46]

Mabel Peel remembered the experience of standing alongside POWs and watching air fights:

> If repairs were needed in our camp, or new hutments were required, it was always the Bosche prisoners who were used for the work, guarded by Tommies. When an air fight was in progress, it was curious for all of us to watch it. The Bosche stopped work immediately, and Tommy, who was far too much of a sport to prevent Fritz from looking on, used to talk over the chances of the fight with him.[47]

Discipline

Concerns about socialising between the sexes were expressed as part of the wider question of discipline. Due to the military versus civilian organisation argument, it was initially a difficult matter and was discussed on both sides of the Channel. On 22 March 1917, Gwynne-Vaughan met with the AG at GHQ, France. Disciplinary options were discussed including court martial for theft and forfeit of pay for unsatisfactory work. Field punishment, where a soldier was tied to a stake, was mentioned and although it was recommended that this should not apply to the WAAC, albeit the associated stoppage of pay should be, nothing was decided at that time.[48] They agreed that the women should not have passes to go out after dark and it was likely that female patrols would be required in larger towns.

The first drafts of women arrived in France before the matter of discipline was resolved. The WAACs were civilians serving the Army and therefore treated as soldiers under military law, which provided for court martial but not for minor punishments. General Instructions No 1, amended by Gwynne-Vaughan, set out a number of punishments but there was no code that detailed which punishments applied in which circumstances. The result was inconsistency between WAAC units and with the Army. On an early inspection, Gwynne-Vaughan asked as usual if the women had any complaints. A worker responded that she had received a heavy punishment for being late for roll call and that she had "'told my friend in the office about it ... and he said that his officer couldn't have done that to him. And please, ma'am, I want to be treated the same as a soldier.'"[49]

Directly as a result of this incident, Gwynne-Vaughan incorporated a code into the Standing Orders for the women in France published in June 1917. The code set out the punishments to be employed by controllers and administrators for minor breaches of discipline: restriction of privileges for up to fourteen days; additional fatigues up to fourteen days; and admonition. Serious breaches were to be reported to the AG. Gwynne-Vaughan was the only one who could stop leave but this did not occur. The key principle was that women were treated in the same way as the men.

The most common misdemeanours perpetrated by the WAACs were: returning late to camp at night without the requisite pass; wearing incorrect uniform; being out of bounds; and socialising with officers. Ruby Ord reflected on her own approach to misdemeanours and discipline: 'we didn't mind being punished for breaking rules we thought were absurd but we did observe the ones we thought were for our safety and welfare and for other people's welfare. I've scrambled through the barbed wire more than once.'[50] Between 1 July 1917 and 11 March 1918 the following punishments were recorded: seventeen fines; forty-one confinements to barracks; twenty-three incidences of restricted privileges; and seven admonitions.[51] The number of individual women to whom these punishments were awarded is not documented.

Fines were introduced as part of the new enrolment in July 1917 and initially awarded by an army officer and only for frequency rather than the nature of the offence. An example is recorded in the War Diary for Director General Transport and General Headquarters Club whereby a worker was awarded a fine of 2/6 by the Camp Commandant for absence without leave and insolence to a forewoman.[52] In the summer of 1918, the responsibility for awarding fines was transferred to the WAAC controllers and administrators.

The class relationship between officials and members was intended to promote discipline. Officials drawn from the middle and upper classes were expected to instil order amongst the lower grades from the working classes. Gwynne-Vaughan's Standing Orders published in June 1917 stated that:

Administrators will adopt towards their subordinates such methods of treatment as will not only ensure respect for authority but also foster the feelings of self-respect and personal honour essential to efficiency. They will be careful to uphold the dignity and authority of those in positions of control subordinate to their own.[53]

Further, propaganda portrayed the officials as motherly figures. Fryniwyd Jesse wrote in March 1918 that '[a] Unit Administrator has to know individually every girl in her camp, though there may be several hundreds. She has to blend with her absolute authority a maternal interest and supervision.'[54]

A number of members referred to the motherly qualities of the officials and spoke of them in glowing terms. Elizabeth Johnston considered that her unit administrator, Miss Lorimer, and her assistant administrator were 'absolutely "it" and sports with a capital "S"'.[55]

However, there were those who were clear about the distinct divide between them. Ruby Ord felt that although most of the officials were pleasant and reasonable they:

didn't appreciate our adulthood, the fact that we were grown-up women. I think they could have done a great deal more for our comfort but they were much more concerned about our being good troops which women never will be.[56]

There were officials who were equally aware of the divide. Dorothy Pickford wrote to her sister that '[a] good many think themselves quite the lady and that sort doesn't take kindly to drill and discipline.'[57]

Officials were selected against the following criteria: high moral tone; experience of the world and therefore not too young; real first-hand knowledge of health questions; knowledge of, and ability to grapple with, moral dangers and evils that may, it was feared, arise where men and women were working together; sound common sense; and the gift of leadership.[58] When visiting France, Marguerite Cody observed that many of the officials had been to public school and university and had very often spent time overseas as the wives of soldiers or civil servants. Promotion of members to officials was rare.

ACI 1069 stated that the power of officials was limited to when the women were off duty or in their hostel. However, later regulations in 1918 stated that no officer or non-commissioned officer could give direct orders to the women and that all communications were to be made through the relevant WAAC administrator.[59] Grievance processes were in place whereby any member who felt aggrieved or considered herself to have been unjustly treated by her superior could submit her case in writing for investigation by the chief controller.[60]

War Diaries

Each area controller, as well as unit administrators attached to GHQ, maintained a War Diary on a daily basis. These are available at the National Archives in London. They include basic information on arrivals, transfers, departures, leave and admittances to hospital, as well as references to key events including inspections and visits. Members are not routinely named but there are some references to individuals. The War Diaries are useful in terms of tracking the appointments and movements of officials. In general, they do not provide an insight into what life was actually like in the WAAC, maintaining an emphasis on logistics. An exception, to a degree, is the War Diary for GHQ 1st Echelon written by Unit Administrator Lilias Ida Gill.[61] For example, on meeting the area controller for Boulogne – Alice Low – she observed that she 'seems a useful sort of person ... and not steeped in this "military attitude for women" mania.'[62] Gwynne-Vaughan also maintained a War Diary in which activities were logged not only by date but also by time of day. It reveals her incredible workload and the amount of travel that she undertook in order to inspect camps herself, as well as be visible to the thousands of women for whom she was responsible. Whilst in France, Marguerite Cody observed of Gwynne-Vaughan that she kept in personal touch with her officials and spoke directly with workers who had received punishment but continued to commit offences.

Chapter 4

Work

Categories of Work

As explained in Chapter 1, the purpose of the WAAC was to substitute women for men in order to free them up for the Front. However, this applied only to specific categories of work that were considered appropriate to women and resulted in many of the WAACs reprising their civilian roles. There are four reasons why this decision was made. First, for the Army it made the enrolment of women into its midst more palatable. As already noted in Chapter 1, Lawson went as far as to say that it would not be right for the men in France to continue to carry out work that was performed in the UK by women. Second, many of the women already had the requisite skills and could therefore take up their work quickly and effectively. Third, there was the belief that women were limited to certain roles due to physical and mental constraints. Finally, it meant a lesser challenge to the existing gendered division of labour. This facilitated the transition of women into the Army in a society that had concerns about the masculinisation of women.

There were eventually seven categories of work in France: Clerical, Household, Mechanical Overseas, Telephone and Postal Overseas, Technical, General Unskilled and Miscellaneous. The levels of substitution were prescribed in the ACIs and regulations, for example four women were considered equivalent to three men in clerical and technical jobs, as well as in the bakeries.[1] Dilution was considered necessary in the more skilled work areas, for example aircraft engine repair, as rather than train a woman to complete all the tasks, which would take years, each could be taught one task and be able to master it quickly. The work of the WAAC was the responsibility of the male officers who employed them and they were overseen by male NCOs.

French women were already working alongside the British Army when the WAAC was established. In March 1917, there were 3,350 French women working for no wage at workshops in the Army Ordnance Department and 430 French women working in the petrol canning installations in Calais and Rouen.[2] In the same month, the AG agreed that, subject to agreement with the Director of Ordnance, the VAD superintendents in the Smoke Helmet Depot could become WAAC officials in charge of the female French labour.[3] French women continued to work with the WAAC in ordnance stores and boot repair workshops, as well as armourer's and wheeler's shops. They also painted camouflage on guns and worked in salvage, where they repaired equipment, for example box respirators.

Gwynne-Vaughan established a school for the Corps in France in January 1918 at which officials and forewomen received training. In the summer of that year it moved to a permanent home in Mesnil-Val next to the WAAC rest camp. The women received training on pay, rations, discipline, drill and physical instruction. They also received information on the military situation, which was provided by an officer from GHQ or the headquarters of one of the armies.[4] Apart from officials and forewomen, the WAACs had no training other than that received on the job. For the most part, they were allocated to a role similar to the one that they had occupied in civilian life.

Specific Roles and Social Class

In his 1916 report, Lawson made direct reference to the type of work that women could carry out and what he considered to be the corresponding social class. He wrote that:

> The class of women will have to be suited to the various employments, ambulance and motor car drivers, clerks, storemen, checkers … and those who work with their heads will naturally be

chosen from the better and educated classes, whereas the cooks, waiters, charwomen, will come from a different stratum.[5]

Indeed, the Corps was established along class lines and the women's position in society was perpetuated within the Corps in terms of the work that they carried out, their grade and their pay. In general, the workers were working and lower-middle class, the forewomen were lower-middle and middle class and the officials were upper-middle and upper class.

In 1918, Edith Barton and Marguerite Cody observed that '[o]ne notable feature of the Army is that all women of the Corps below the grade corresponding to Army officers are treated in exactly the same way. There is no feeling of class distinction.'[6] However, this was not the experience of many of the women. Elsie Cooper recalled that:

> I think there was [sic] around a thousand in the camp and each part was separated. The telephonists had one part, the clerical and the shorthand typists had another part and the household were entirely separate. We didn't know the household girls or hardly any of them, only the ones who served us. I don't think they were very pleased to serve us, either.[7]

The WAACs worked in a variety of locations, from the docks through to the Officers Clubs, base camps, WAAC camps, GHQ, Records Offices, as well as latterly in Schools of Instruction in the Army Areas. They were attached to the Tank Corps Reinforcement Park at Le Tréport, the RFC (latterly RAF) at Pont-de-l'Arche, the Royal Engineers at Aire, war worker hostels in Gézaincourt and Blendeques and the AEF. As well as the more standard roles as clerks, cooks and drivers, a minority undertook a range of specialist roles, for example with Army Intelligence and the Ordnance Survey and as gardeners and printers. The following are examples of the jobs undertaken by the women.

Motor Drivers

The motor drivers of the Mechanical Overseas Section were generally middle class. These women had often learned to drive before the war and were able to afford the required training in driving and motor mechanics run by private companies, e.g. the British School of Motoring (BSM). The drivers were required to have at least six months experience in driving heavy vehicles. It is incorrectly stated in some secondary sources that the WAACs drove ambulances. This was, in fact, the responsibility of the VAD General Service Section, whose drivers were usually from the upper classes. Many of the WAAC drivers were based at the AMTD in Abbeville, which was also staffed by WAAC clerks.

They initially experienced negativity from the men, for example finding that their tyres had been let down, as this was one of the jobs least associated with women, but they were eventually accepted. Dolly Shepherd, a WAAC driver, remembered that when she had to fix a car at the garage for the first time, all the men stopped work to watch her. Coincidentally, it was a task that she had completed as part of her mechanics exam in the UK. The men cheered when she successfully completed the work. On another occasion, she came across a major whose car had broken down. She offered her help but the chauffeur claimed that she would not be able to fix it. She persisted and managed to get the vehicle running again by using one of her hairpins as an improvised tool. The next morning a cup of milk was left out for her as a thank you.[8]

The WAAC drivers were also exposed to considerable danger as they drove close to the Front, even though this was not officially sanctioned. Dolly Shepherd once took an army ordnance officer to repair a gun right behind the line. She saw the grey uniformed Germans, as well as a number of British soldiers running away. She recalled that they were arrested and she cried on the journey home knowing that they would be shot.[9] The second photograph at plate three shows three WAACs working on a motor car in France. This photograph was one of many taken for the Ministry of Information to be used at home and overseas for propaganda purposes.

Clerks and Signallers

The signallers (telephonists and telegraphists) wore a blue and white armband and were sometimes referred to as the blue and white angels. They were used as substitutes for men at exchanges at the bases, as well as in depots and camps. The men that they replaced carried out signalling work further up the line. It was a pressurised environment in which accuracy was required and the highly skilled WAACs worked in shifts to operate the exchanges on a twenty-four hour basis. The women were also required to deal with a significant amount of sensitive information and signed a statement that they would not divulge outside of the office any information relating to their work. Many of the telephonists were required to speak French so that they could communicate with the French telephone exchanges.

The signallers were drawn from the Civil Service and were generally from the lower-middle class. Consequently, there were differences between them and the other workers. Annie Martin described her experience of first joining the WAAC as follows:

> We mixed with a very different set of women altogether. There were any amount of women going out to be bakers … and their life and their attitude to life was very different to ours. For instance, it was communal washing … well my friend and I we stripped to the waist every morning to wash, we always had done … but these people from Glasgow … they never washed 'til they were fully dressed and they washed above their collars. They were horrified, they thought we were indecent.[10]

She stated that the signallers did not really mix with 'the others'.

Elizabeth Johnston made reference to class in one of her letters home just before she left for France, writing:

I should be quite alarmed to hear of any member of our family joining the W.A.A.C. or anyone who has been brought up to refinement … . You come into the closest contact with the very worst types. They are thieving every day, and we are all warned to carry our valuables on our person. So far I've had nothing stolen. … You simply must make a stand and keep it, but deal very gently and tactfully with the 'Arriets.[11]

'Arriet was the name she used to refer to the working class women. However, in the same letter she wrote that:

There are, fortunately, girls of the highest order here, the very finest types of womanhood and the essence of refinement. Most of these have sense enough to look on from a humorous standpoint. They are truly to be pitied, who look down their noses, and draw in their skirts, while they give thanks they are not as other women are.[12]

In her letters, Elizabeth may have made reference to the differences between herself and a number of her colleagues but she made every effort to get along with them and was aware of how they viewed her. Indeed, one of the stated aims of the Adult School that she joined at the Calais camp was '[t]o bring together in helpful comradeship and active service the different classes of society.'[13]

The clerks were also from the lower-middle class. Their skills, developed in their civilian employment, were transferable but they were required to learn the language of the Army and in some cases, for example Motor Transport Depots and Ordnance Depots, this was relatively technical. However, this would equally have been a challenge for a man with no experience in these areas of the Army. A significant number of WAAC clerks were employed at the Army Records Office based in a thirteenth century Archbishop's Palace in Rouen. The women updated and filed records of every man serving in the Army in France, as well as for their own Corps. Several hundred clerks were also attached to the Army Pay Office in Wimereux and maintained the pay records of every man in the Army in France.

Cooks and Waitresses

The cooks and waitresses were from the working classes. Many of the cooks had transferred from the Cookery Section of the Women's Legion and the majority had obtained qualifications in domestic science. The cooks and waitresses worked in the Officers Clubs, canteens, messes and Army Schools, as well as the WAAC camps and hostels. The WAACs in other sections, for example clerks, often ate with the men during the day. This meant the preparation of four meals a day for thousands of men and women, as well as the subsequent washing up. The kitchens operated very long hours, in some bases for twenty-four hours a day, but the cooks and waitresses worked in shifts. The WAAC cooks were very popular with the base commanders. Marguerite Cody was told by one officer that:

> they are most decidedly better than the average soldier cook. For one thing they are cleaner, and for another there is no chance of their getting drunk, and little likelihood of their stealing the things that pass through their hands.[14]

The WAAC was also credited with making efficiency savings, not only in terms of the number of women replacing men which was often fewer with regards to cooks, but also the decrease in actual spend. This had first been observed when the Women's Legion cooks began work in army camps in the UK. In one camp the daily messing of an officer was reduced from 2/6 to -/9 a day. In addition to saving money, the WAAC cooks sent home the fat saved during cooking on the Soyer stoves for use in the munitions industry.

There is very little information available in the primary sources about the cooks and waitresses in their own words.

Intelligence

In September 1917, the Intelligence Department of the War Office began the recruitment of women into the Intelligence Corps. They required fluent German speakers who could decode intercepted communications. The women were recruited into the WAAC and on 28 September 1917, six assistant administrators left the UK for the Intelligence Branch of the General Staff at St Omer, France. They were some of the few officials that replaced army officers. One of the women, Mabel Peel, wrote in her memoir of the day they left the Connaught Club:

> We had a good send-off … as we had attained a certain amount of dignity and prestige from the fact that we were going out to do some mysterious work, the nature of which we knew no more than anyone else.[15]

Indeed, the women did not know the exact nature of their work until their first day in the office. Mabel Peel noted that:

> I think none of us will ever forget that first morning at the office, when we sat there, with sheets of paper in front of us on which were arranged in the form of sentences, meaningless groups of letters. We were told that they were codes, wireless messages (coming from the Germans and tapped by our operators). We were to try and solve them. Never having seen a code message in our lives before, you can imagine the despair that filled our hearts. … On discussing the work at lunch time, which we had to do in very guarded terms because of the presence of the orderlies, we found a certain amount of consolation in the fact that everyone was as depressed about it all as everyone else, and each felt as dull witted and stupid as the others.[16]

The women soon became effective in their role. Mabel Peel recalled that:

We began to find our work intensely interesting, and as we began to see more and more daylight in it, found it monopolising all our thoughts both waking and sleeping. … I know that at the end of three months, a colleague and myself decoded our daily messages quite by ourselves, handing up our suggestions each evening to be signed by the head of the room.[17]

A measure of their contribution is not available among the primary sources but the messages that they decoded did include those related to troop movements. The women, nicknamed the 'Hush WAACs,' worked long hours, including on Sundays and had one half day off a week when they stopped work at 1600. After May 1918, they were permitted to have one day off a month. The women slept in a separate part of the camp and had their own staff. Their camp was subjected to bombing raids and in April 1918, with the advance of the Germans, the Hush WAACs were moved to Le Touquet where they lived in the Villa Joyeuse until the Armistice. Gwynne-Vaughan, in her autobiography, wrote sparingly of these women, stating that she believed they translated and prepared documents and that the Corps knew little of what they did.[18] It may be that Gwynne-Vaughan did not want to reveal any detail relatively soon after events, but Mabel Peel had already published her account, albeit sanitised, in 1921.

Ordnance Survey and Printers
In November 1917, the Ordnance Survey moved from Southampton to a factory building by the canal in Wardrecques, near St Omer in France. It became the Overseas Branch of the Ordnance Survey (OBOS) led by Lieutenant Colonel William James Johnston. One hundred and three male civilians who worked in the Ordnance Survey in the UK joined the Corps of Royal Engineers and transferred to OBOS. They were followed in March 1918 by forty-six of their female colleagues who enrolled with the WAAC. The women worked shifts of eight hours on and eight hours off. One of the women described the heavy workload:

The maps had to be printed ... and I worked on the machine ... used to do a thousand maps an hour. And we weren't allowed to get down because we had to work all the time until somebody came to relieve us.[19]

One million maps were produced by OBOS during the time it was located in Wardrecques. OBOS was evacuated in the spring of 1918 and moved to Aubengue near Boulogne. Shortly after the evacuation, the location where the WAACs had previously been living was bombed.

All printing for the Army, for example of orders and instructions, was carried out in France. Although there were women who had experience in the trade at home, very few had worked linotype printing presses due to trade union rule. For the most part, therefore, the WAACs were employed to carry out the less skilled work such as folding, binding and working the perforating machine. In 1918, Marguerite Cody visited the army printers in Abbeville and noted that:

Within a few weeks of their arrival, their output in a day exceeded by four times the amount done by the men they replaced. The officer in command has "requisitioned" fourteen or fifteen more WAACs from England, proof positive that he is more than satisfied with his present women workers ...[20]

Gardeners

The Graves Registration Commission was incorporated into the Army in 1915 and became the Imperial War Graves Commission in May 1917. In April 1917, Chalmers Watson met with General Fabian Ware, the founder of the Commission, and Arthur Hill, Assistant Director at Kew Gardens. The objective was to discuss the supply of women to work in the military cemeteries in France.[21] The initial requirement was for seventy women, with two to three women at each cemetery. Arthur Hill was concerned that the women would find the work lonely but agreed to discuss the matter with Gwynne-Vaughan in France the following week. All agreed that the women should have some horticultural experience. Gwynne-Vaughan met with two officers of the Imperial War Graves Commission on 4 June 1917.[22] In July 1917, the War Office sent a request to the Department of National Service for twenty women gardeners. The request went as far as to name five horticultural colleges which may have been a source of such women.[23] The Department of National Service contacted a number of these establishments and asked them to get in touch with past students, as well as placing newspaper advertisements. A Selection Board was held in London on 19 July 1917 and successful applicants sent to France.

Members of the WAAC, working under the Commission, maintained the graves of the fallen. They did not dig graves – this was done by the men – but they filled them in, sowed grass, planted trees and roses, tended them and laid wreathes sent by families at home. They also attended the funerals. Nora Barker was one of the gardeners who joined in July 1917. She was interviewed by Arthur Hill and remembered that he seemed rather embarrassed, as men did not interview women. Her application was successful and she worked at the Abbeville and Wimereux Cemeteries. The women worked hard as there were many burials. Nora Barker recalled that '[w]e had runners up every afternoon from the different hospitals, there were a lot of hospitals around, with notes to say how many there would be the next morning.'[24] When asked how she related to the graves, for example looking at the names and ages on the wooden crosses, she replied that she didn't look at them and that '[i]t was part of a job and that was that.'[25] She also confirmed that she did not find her work depressing and it did not give her satisfaction.

On 2 March 1918, the *Illustrated London News* published a drawing by Frederic de Haenen based on an official photograph[26] (first image at plate three). It depicted a group of WAACs tending graves and laying a wreath with the words 'To Fred – From Mother and All.' This drawing would have been intended to provide comfort to those at home. It may also have been a way of emphasising the caring nature of the WAACs, a trait traditionally associated with the female, as a counterpoint to the controversy surrounding the WAAC at the time (see Chapter 6).

G R

WOMEN
URGENTLY WANTED
for the

W·A·A·C

WOMEN'S ARMY
AUXILIARY CORPS

WORK AT HOME
AND ABROAD
WITH THE FORCES

COOKS CLERKS
WAITRESSES
DRIVER-MECHANICS

ALL KINDS *of* DOMESTIC WORKERS
& WOMEN *in* MANY OTHER CAPACITIES
TO TAKE THE PLACE OF MEN

GOOD WAGES ▼ QUARTERS
UNIFORM RATIONS

FOR ALL INFORMATION & ADVICE APPLY AT
NEAREST EMPLOYMENT EXCHANGE
THE ADDRESS CAN BE OBTAINED AT ANY POST OFFICE

1. Ministry of Labour recruitment poster for the WAAC. © *Imperial War Museums (Q 68242)*

2. *The Workers' Quarters, Queen Mary's Army Auxiliary Corps: Queen Elizabeth Camp, Vendroux* by Beatrice Lithiby. © *Imperial War Museums (Art.IWM ART 2904)*

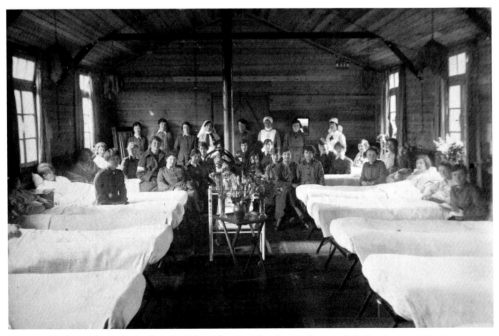

3. WAACs in a ward attached to the Sick Sisters' Hospital in Rouen. (*Author's own collection*)

4. *Tending the Graves of Our Heroes: Gardeners of the WAAC* by Frederic de Haenen, *Illustrated London News*, 2 March 1918. (*Author's own collection*)

5. WAAC mechanics working on a motor car in France. (*Author's own collection*)

I've never been wounded, but I've had an awful W.A.A.C. on the knee!

6. Comic postcard by Doug Tempest, 1918. © *Bamforth and Co. Ltd.*

7. Crater at Abbeville WAAC camp, 22 May 1918. © *Imperial War Museums (Q 7890)*

8. WAACs sleeping in the open in Crécy Forest, 7 June 1918. © *Imperial War Museums (Q 11065)*

9. Jeanie Watson prior to enrolment with the WAAC. © *L. McNulty*

10. Jeanie Watson in her WAAC uniform. © *L. McNulty*

11. WAAC and QMAAC badges within the commemorative window at Guildford Cathedral. (*Author's own collection and reproduced with kind permission of Guildford Cathedral*)

12. Statue of *Faith* located externally to the commemorative window at Guildford Cathedral. (*Author's own collection and reproduced with kind permission of Guildford Cathedral*)

Fryniwyd Jesse referred to the way in which the care given by the WAAC gardeners for the dead followed on from that provided by the women at home to keep men well, and of the nurses who provided succour when they were ill.[27]

American Expeditionary Force

To save shipping space, the AEF arrived in France with the minimum of administrative personnel. The initial use of English speaking French and Belgian women, as well as unskilled American men, to operate the telephone exchanges was not successful. General Pershing, Commander in Chief, AEF in France, asked for women to be sent from the US to work as telephone operators and eventually his request was met. The first unit of female operators attached to the American Army Signal Corps and referred to as 'Hello Girls', arrived in France on 24 March 1918. Six months later, thirteen female telephone operators were sent to work in exchanges located at the Front in the villages of Ligny and Souilly. The women were enrolled as civilians and did not receive Victory medals until 1979.

General Pershing also identified a need for female clerks and workers in the American Central Records Office and American Central Post Office, but the American War Department would not agree to send women to France from the US to fill these posts. Consequently, General Pershing approached the British War Office with a request for 5,000 British women to work as clerks with the AEF in France. On 10 June 1918, a conference was held between the WAAC (Florence Leach), the WRNS and the Employment Department to discuss the request.[28] At this point a number of officials, including Hilda Horniblow of the WAAC, were also making enquiries in France. Florence Leach did not want to make it known to recruits at the application stage that they may work with the AEF, rather that suitable women be chosen after selection. In this way she hoped to recruit 'a good class of girl.'[29] This suggests that she believed that openly recruiting women to work with the AEF may have attracted some women for the wrong reasons but she did not specifically state what those reasons would have been. Although non-British women were not able to work in the WAAC, the possibility of contacting American women in the UK was discussed as they would be able to work with the AEF. There is no evidence that this approach was taken.

In July 1918, two representatives from the War Office travelled to Le Havre to discuss the detail of how the WAAC would be drafted to the AEF. The deputy controller at Le Havre – Alice Low – was to be responsible for the drafts when they arrived in France at the new camp that had been established for them in nearby Harfleur. The first draft was convened at the camp on 9 July 1918 and arrived at the AEF base in Tours on 11 July 1918. Tours was the location of one of the AEFs key telephone exchanges, as well as the American Central Records Office. Approximately 200 WAACs were attached to the AEF at this time. They had their own chief controller and Hilda Horniblow filled the post. As there were two chief controllers in France, Florence Leach was promoted to Controller in Chief in July 1918 and Violet Long to Chief Controller. Hilda Horniblow later returned to the UK to take up the post made vacant by the death of Violet Long as a result of the torpedoing of the *Warilda* in August 1918. Violet Long had accompanied a draft of WAACs from the UK to work with the AEF. She had been returning home to provide a full report to her sister, Florence Leach, on the WAACs working with the AEF. Hilda Horniblow was replaced by L.M. Gordon and the post was subsequently downgraded from Chief Controller.

In August 1918, the newspapers reported that 5,000 women were required to work with the WAAC alongside the AEF in France and invited women to apply at their local Employment Exchange.

In September 1918, the American Central Records Office moved to Bourges and the majority of the WAACs in Tours went with it. The Records Office was housed in the old barracks at Caserne Carnot. The number of WAACs attached to the AEF reached approximately 500, which was significantly less than the 5,000 originally requested. The Records Office included the Locator Card Section, which held an index card for each AEF soldier. The WAACs maintained details of a soldier's location and provided families with details of where fallen soldiers were buried. The WAACs were inspected by General Pershing on at least one occasion. They were also visited by the American author and poet Ella Wheeler Wilcox, who went on a lecture tour of Allied Forces camps in 1918.

Six WAAC administrators worked in Paris with the AEF at the Labour Bureau, which was based at the Champs Élysées Palace Hotel.

There are varying descriptions of the relationship between the WAACs and the Americans. Charlotte Bottomley did not work with the AEF but she was told not to mix with them socially as 'they were … very keen on women … and we'd be getting into bother if we mixed with the Americans … we were put against them.'[30] Annie Martin said that the WAACs liked the individual Americans very much but were not keen on their views after the war:

> the thing that struck us most then was that they thought they'd come over here and absolutely won the war. I went for a tour of the battlefields with a mixed crowd, including some Americans and everywhere the Americans – this is where we won so and so.[31]

The American authorities were very complimentary of the WAAC. The women found it more difficult to adjust to the Americans than vice versa. Colonel Julia Cowper and Roy Terry refer to the fact that the AEF was not as strict as the British Army and that the women preferred the latter.[32]

General Orders No 46 issued by Colonel David L. Stone, Commanding Headquarters, AEF, Bourges on 27 June 1919 marked the end of the WAAC service with the Records Office in Bourges.[33] The orders were very complimentary of the WAAC, both in terms of the quality of their work and engagement in sporting events and entertainment. The same day, AG Davis of the AEF wired Florence Leach for her assistance in retaining the 300 WAACs at the Records Office for a further month.[34] The War Office sent a telegram authorising the retention of the women for two weeks but it arrived too late. On 29 June 1919, the AG telegraphed Colonel Stone to advise him that he had been made aware that arrangements had already been made for the transfer out of the women and this should continue as planned. Colonel Stone subsequently wrote to Florence Leach apologising for the confusion.[35]

On 3 July 1919, in response to the emotional tone of General Orders No 46, Florence Leach wrote an equally emotional letter to Colonel Stone. She thanked him for the way in which the WAAC had been received and accepted, writing:

> Had it not been for the splendid spirit of good fellowship and co-operation, which was shown to us in the beginning and throughout our service with the American Army, I feel sure that the universal feeling of sadness and regret at their departure, which I found at Bourges and Tours, would not have been so marked.[36]

After the war, an illuminated letter of thanks from the Director General of Transportation, AEF, ended up being hung on the wall of the QMAAC Old Comrades Association (OCA) headquarters in London.

Royal Air Force and Women's Royal Air Force

WAACs worked at the RFC (latterly RAF) Engine Repair Shops at Pont-de-l'Arche from the summer of 1917. The extensive site included a canteen, dance hall and café. The work that the women carried out was technical and included acetylene welding and operating metal lathes.

In April 1918, the RAF and WRAF were formed. The latter was headed by Violet Douglas-Pennant. Officials and members of the WAAC and WRNS, as well as members of the Women's Legion Motor Drivers, employed with RAF units, were permitted to volunteer to transfer to the WRAF. Where possible they remained attached to the unit in which they had already been working. Those who chose not to transfer were re-posted within their own corps after 1 July 1918.[37] The women at Pont-de-l'Arche, however, remained in the WAAC and worked at the site until 1919.

Officials

The work of the officials was focussed on the efficient running of hostels and of the Corps and included inspections, drill, roll call, accounts, letter censoring, issuing passes and maintaining discipline. They were required to ensure adherence to general routine orders, standing orders and instructions. Unit administrators provided weekly reports to the area controller and included the total number of women by grade and work category, a brief summary of passes given, punishments and casualties, as well as details of any problems that had arisen regarding health, conduct and general welfare.

*   *   *

Daily Routine

The women's daily routine differed dependent on their work and location. By reviewing a range of primary and secondary sources it is possible to compile the following broad timetable:

Between 0700 and 0750	Reveille and Roll Call
Between 0745 and 0800	Breakfast
1300	Dinner
Between 1630 and 1900	Tea
Between 2000 and 2015	Workers back in camp
Between 2000 and 2100	Roll call
2100	Officials and forewomen back in camp
Between 2100 and 2230	Lights out

Timetables were posted on the wall in the camp or hostel and each meal effectively acted as a roll call. The women were expected to attend church parade and service on Sundays.

Working hours were long and the women had little time off. It varied from one day off in seven to a half day one week and every other Sunday. They were entitled to two weeks paid leave each year, with a free travel warrant to their home in the UK. Free travel to and from France was only permitted once every six months. Controllers and administrators were permitted to travel first class but all others were required to travel third class. In comparison to male soldiers, there was a certain amount of flexibility, for example compassionate leave was available for women who were needed at home due to sickness in the family. Exceptionally, a woman could be discharged in these circumstances. Marguerite Cody noted Gwynne-Vaughan's attitude that 'a girl's position in her home, so very different from that of a man, must be recognised, and allowance made for it.'[38] In August 1918, the War Office proposed to increase the leave allowance for WAACs in France to ten days in each six months. This was due to the 'constant sights and sounds of war prevalent in France, to which women serving overseas are subject, and of the feeling of greater distance from home.'[39] This proposed change was not accepted. In 1919, as part of an effort to retain women, the leave allowance was increased to thirty-three days.

Pay

The WAACs were not paid at the same rate as the male soldiers. Dilution, whereby a number of women took on the role of one man, was used as an argument for this.

The Civil Service based WAAC pay on a civilian model but this was modified over time. Initially, it was decided that domestic workers would be paid by the year but others, for example drivers and clerks, would be paid by the week (forty-two to forty-eight hours dependent on the category of work) plus overtime. This was set out in ACI 537 published in March 1917. However, at a conference convened by the

Secretary of State on 25 May 1917, it was agreed that overtime was to be abolished and this was incorporated in ACI 1069 published in July 1917.

ACI 1069 set out the rates of pay for each work category. These were dependent on the women re-enrolling, which was another requirement of that ACI. As stated in Chapter 2, this resulted in a loss of pay for some categories due to the removal of overtime. For example, under ACI 537, a telephonist received 28/- for a forty-eight hour week with overtime of -/8 (weekdays) and -/10 (Sundays)[40] but under ACI 1069 she was paid a flat rate of 28/- and no overtime.[41] As a result, some women resisted re-enrolment. Under ACI 537, the women were to receive a £5 bonus after one year of service, as well as a proportionate sum for subsequent service. Under ACI 1069, however, no bonus was to be issued to new recruits and only those who enrolled prior to July 1917 were eligible to receive the payment.

ACI 1069 also set out the pay for officials. This ranged from £450 for the chief controller overseas to £120 for deputy and assistant administrators.[42]

The National Service Department had raised concerns in the summer of 1917 that the number of women willing to accept a lower rate of pay as long as they could work in France was declining. In addition, women clerks in the WAAC in London received a higher rate of pay than those in France and the rest of the UK, and other categories received a lower rate at home than in France. The National Service Department recommended that an Immobile section be formed which would include all WAACs serving in the UK not liable to be moved from their home, and that they be paid a flat rate, rather than a local rate dependent on where they lived. The flat rate would be the same for service either at home or overseas. Until this point all women had been recruited as Mobile. The term Mobile continued to apply to women who could be transferred within the UK, as well as those serving in France. The recommendation was forwarded by the Army Council to the Treasury in December 1917 who concurred and the matter was submitted to the Labour Co-ordinating Committee.[43] The Immobile Branch was established in January 1918.

The *Regulations for the Queen Mary's Army Auxiliary Corps*, published in June 1918, set out the rates of pay for each work category. The Clerical, Mechanical and Technical categories were the highest paid. Clerical ranged from 27/6 to 45/- per week dependent on grade, Mechanical from 35/- to 40/- and Technical from 24/- to 42/-.[44] The lowest paid categories were General Unskilled with a range from 24/- to 30/- a week and Household from 9/- to 17/- a week.[45] At this time, a number of proposals regarding pay increases in a number of jobs, for example clerks and printer's assistants, were put to the Co-ordinating Conference on Women's Corps and accepted.[46] The conference, attended by representatives of the WAAC, WRNS, WRAF and VAD General Service Section, was convened on a weekly basis from June 1918 to discuss terms of service, uniform etc. and ensure consistency across the Women's Services.

Household, or domestic workers, received free board, lodging and service (i.e. cooking). Initially they were paid -/6 a week to arrange to have their personal clothes laundered but later this was done for them for 1/6. Non-domestic members had 14/- a week deducted for washing, service and food. For officials, this was 15/6. For members this included laundry of eight pieces of personal clothing in addition to their issue work clothing. Officials, however, were required to arrange this for themselves.[47] Emily Rumbold recalled that:

My pay was 20/- on paper, 14/- was taken away for keep ... and -/18 of that went for laundry. But it was no good sending to the Army laundry so we sent our own laundry to French people ... to little private cottages ... we had to pay for it ourselves ... and the Army still took the -/18.[48]

Taking the deductions into account, the domestic workers had the least money in their pockets at the end of the week. The WAACs were expected to pay for their own shoe repairs and to replace their stockings, for which they received a renewal grant of £1.

Any officials and members whose pay did not exceed £250 per year were entitled to sick pay. If the injury or sickness was directly attributable to their service and certified by a Medical Board, they received three months full pay. This was followed by three quarters pay for three months and then half pay subject to War Office approval.

The women were in the payment of the unit to which they were attached and their commanding officer was required to countersign the attendance book for the women on a daily basis. Elizabeth Johnston wrote in her diary of the joy that she felt on receiving her first pay:

> my army paybook being endorsed, "In the Field!" I had thrills, and throughout the morning had frequent peeps at my paybook, reading and re-reading the magic words. When I think of my regimental number, my army shoes (!) and my identification disc, I positively feel thrilled! And now I've an army paybook endorsed by my paying officer "In the Field, January 5th, 1918!!"[49]

At the end of September 1918, the War Office wrote to the Treasury on behalf of the Army Council requesting an increase in pay for WAAC administrators of different grades. The request was based on the fact that the pay had been fixed since 1917 and many of their civilian counterparts had received bonuses.[50] They were supported in their request by the Air Force and Admiralty.

In October 1918, the Treasury replied to the War Office, refusing to award a pay rise to WAAC administrators on the grounds that they received board and lodging at a fixed charge. They did agree to a pay increase to deputy administrators as they acknowledged that the women had increased responsibilities, often responsible for the women in their charge for twenty-four hours a day. A note on the front of the file shows that the Treasury was concerned that if a pay increase was sanctioned there would subsequently be a request to increase the pay of the lower grades.[51]

Following the Armistice, the War Office replied to the Treasury stating that it would not pursue the request for a pay increase but changes were needed so that the WAAC was treated in the same way as the WRAF and WRNS. These changes included increasing the salary of deputy administrators in hostels with more than 200 women.[52] The Treasury replied a month later, on 8 January 1919, agreeing to the proposals.

Despite the War Office not pursuing the original proposals for a pay increase for administrators after the Armistice, they requested an increase in November 1918 for domestic workers in the WAAC, as well as the VAD General Service Section. WAAC domestic workers, other than head cooks, had not had an increase since January 1917. The initial response was negative, as the Treasury understood that recruiting had ceased and demobilisation was to take place as soon as possible. In March 1919, the War Office pushed the matter again as out-of-work donation pay was higher than the pay for WAAC domestic workers and the men in France were paid a bonus. An internal Treasury memo reveals that they considered the pay of WAAC domestic workers to be higher as they received board and lodging for a rate of 14/-, which was lower than the market rate. However, they acknowledged that the women had enrolled for twelve months or the duration and that although demobilisation was the answer there were the subsequent unemployment fears and the need for the women to stay on so that the men could be demobilised first.[53] In April 1919, the Treasury agreed to the pay rises for the WAAC domestic workers, including 2/- to cooks and general domestic workers and 1/6 to assistant forewomen cooks and waitresses.[54]

Chapter 5

Controversy

Rumours at Home and in France

In August 1917, the papers reported on the publication of ACI 1069 the previous month and provided complimentary updates on the progress of the WAAC. These included details of how the women were allowed to mix with the men, albeit balancing this with the disciplinary procedures to which the women were subject. A few months later, however, they published a statement issued by Sir Auckland Geddes in response to rumours in British society of moral danger in France:

> To anxious, and rightly anxious, parents let me say that, though life in the W.A.A.C. is neither lazy nor luxurious, the girls and women in the corps are well looked after and there is certainly no need for any one of them to get into trouble. I would far sooner see my own daughter in the ranks of the W.A.A.C. than in a big office or a munition factory so far as supervision and the risk of exposure to undesirable influences are concerned.[1]

In spite of the positive press reporting which carried on into early 1918, all levels of society maintained a generally negative view of the WAAC. The reasons remained the same as when the Corps was established but in 1918 the focus shifted towards morality. More information was available on the environment in which the women lived and worked, which fuelled the imagination. The British public was aware that the WAACs and soldiers were officially allowed to mix outside of working hours. Further, there were reports of the spread of venereal disease amongst soldiers through the use of prostitutes, resulting in many considering France to be a den of iniquity. In February 1918, the Association for Moral and Social Hygiene issued a statement, which was widely circulated, on immorality in France. It claimed that brothels had been opened in Cayeux and Le Havre near convalescent camps for British soldiers and that one had been sanctioned by the British Army.

As set out in Chapter 2, one of the reasons for the early dislike of the WAAC was its foundation in the working classes. In the UK, a connection had already been made by some between questionable morality and working class and lower-middle class women engaged in traditionally male jobs or war work. This was extended to the WAAC, particularly those serving overseas. The morality of the VADs, who came from the upper classes, was not questioned. Neither was that of nurses, who were seen as carrying out a traditional female role in wartime. The WAACs, who were challenging traditional gendered wartime roles, were seen as posing a threat to the morality of the men.

There were those in the UK who believed that women were joining the WAAC with the sole purpose of going to France for immoral purposes. Gwynne-Vaughan was aware of only one woman who joined the WAAC to work as a prostitute in France. The woman was caught leaving the camp after roll call but, due to the system of fines, she had to be caught three times before removal to the UK. Interestingly, there were those who believed the opposite of the WAACs, i.e. they were too masculine.

An alternative image of the WAAC to that in the press was portrayed in popular culture. The postcard on plate four, printed in 1918, illustrates a famous joke of the time: 'I may not have been wounded but I've had an awful WAAC on the knee.'

The questioning of WAAC morality had a particular impact on the wives, fiancées and sweethearts of men serving overseas. They would likely have experienced a range of emotions from concern to sexual jealousy.

As explained in Chapter 3, the Army did have early concerns about the mixing of soldiers and WAACs but agreed that they should do so with official approval. The WAAC administrators, from the middle and upper classes, were expected to control the workers. It was not the role of the male army officers to whom the women worked.

The soldiers quickly grew accustomed to the WAACs, but there were those who did not respect them or their reasons for enrolling. In March 1918, the government issued a new order under the Defence of the Realm Act (DORA), which made it an offence to communicate a venereal disease to a soldier. A minority of soldiers subsequently made unfounded claims against the WAAC. There were also soldiers who believed that the women had gone out to France to prostitute themselves. One soldier, Robert Cude, recorded in his diary his views of the WAACs that he met in France:

I have no hesitation in saying, that to my mind, they are a disgrace to the country they belong to. There are good among them, but the good are over shadowed by the bad. Girls, I prefer to give them another name.[2]

Charlotte Bottomley encountered one such soldier when she went on leave to London. At Victoria Station she had:

a spot of bother with a soldier standing on the platform, who passed some derogatory remarks about the WAACs. ... He hinted that we were more or less prostitutes sent out to amuse the Army, which naturally I took exception to and stood up to him and told him off. A crowd gathered ... and the Military Police were called ... and told me to take off the blue and white armband from my coat. ... I refused to do this as it was part of my uniform ... . By the time I returned to Abbeville ... the unit administrator had the whole case before her. But when I explained my side of the row she said that I had acted on behalf of my comrades in defending our good name.[3]

The WAACs were aware that many of the French civilians believed that they were camp followers and prostitutes. The French referred to them as 'Les Soldates' and 'Les Tomettes'. There was no equivalent to the WAAC in France and they were viewed variously as novelties or women of questionable morals. Annie Martin observed that:

> in the opinion of the French there was only one reason why the women had been sent out and that was for comforts for the troops. … They were hostile to the women to an extent, they thought we had gone out there for one purpose only and we were undercutting the French women.[4]

A number of WAACs reported that local children would use the phrase 'jig a jig one franc' within earshot.

It was against this backdrop that specific rumours about WAAC prostitution and pregnancy began to spread in France, as well as at home. They were not propagated by the press. One rumour was supposed to have been started by a soldier carrying out guard duty outside what he alleged to be a WAAC maternity home. Chalmers Watson wrote to Gwynne-Vaughan describing the rumours that she had heard, which included £50 bonuses being paid to WAACs who became pregnant and state adoption of babies born to WAACs.

As early as December 1917, officials in the WAAC and Ministry of Labour discussed the possibility of the War Office instigating proceedings against individuals who spread false rumours.[5] In the same month, Miss L.C. Hague, a teacher in Ilkeston, Derbyshire was dismissed by the Board of Governors. She was accused of distributing pacifist literature and also of slandering the WAAC. The War Office subsequently stated that anyone spreading false accusations about the WAAC, which were prejudicial to recruitment, would be treated as an offender under DORA.

Gwynne-Vaughan, who had briefly returned to the UK, sought to dispel the rumours at the recruiting meetings that she attended. She explained that to separate the women from the men would have inferred that they were not to be trusted and that allowing them to mix had resulted in a sensible comradeship. In February 1918, Frances

Durham of the Ministry of Labour wrote to AG11 requesting a definitive statement that could be used for general publicity and that the Ministry of Labour, with reference to the War Office, would deal with any negative press reports that may arise.[6]

There were pregnancies amongst the WAACs at a rate of fewer than three per thousand per year. However, every case was reported by Gwynne-Vaughan to the AG and she provided details of the dates of each woman's condition. In most cases the women were either pregnant when they enrolled or fell pregnant after marrying while in service. The women were discharged on compassionate grounds. The pregnancies were not a secret and therefore the WAACs in France were aware of incidences amongst their colleagues and that the rate of pregnancy was low. Charlotte Bottomley stated that:

> We also had our share of girls who went off the straight and narrow. I think we had about four or five sent back to England to have babies which isn't bad considering the number of personnel which passed through Camp 3 in roughly two years.[7]

Nora Barker recalled that her father was 'rather ashamed of me because there was a lot of scandal going on about the WAACs overseas, hundreds of them coming back being pregnant mothers.'[8] However, she did not experience any ill feeling from the public when she returned home.

George Roberts (Minister for Labour), gave a number of speeches supporting the WAAC, stating that the government was trying to trace the origin of the allegations of improper conduct and that there was no truth in them.

There were many in official circles that defended the WAAC. The Archbishop of Canterbury, who had visited the Corps in France in 1917, gave a speech on the 5 February 1918 in the Upper House of Convocation at Church House in London. In relation to the stories about widespread immorality and harm in connection with the WAAC, he stated that:

Those stories were absolutely untrue. [He] had gone to the very bottom of it and found the allegations to be entirely untrue. … The moral standard among these women workers was extremely high, the control exceedingly good, and the whole thing was very well done. [He] was lost in admiration at the way in which the rules for the members of the WAAC had been planned and the way in which effect was given to those rules. [He] had been greatly struck by the way in which the War Office authorities were giving the best possible help in the way of guiding, protecting from mischief, and encouraging for good the thousands of women and girls who were going out to the front.[9]

The *Edinburgh Evening News*, in response to the Archbishop, wrote that enemy agents were being given too much credit for starting the rumours and that it would be better to investigate what was happening in the women's ranks. It also suggested that a number of the women had found the life harder than expected and become disillusioned.[10]

The following day, in the Upper House of Convocation, the Archbishop of Canterbury is reported to have said, regarding brothels in France, that:

Although he had described the stories of immorality among the women workers with the Army abroad as being terribly exaggerated, he was by no means prepared to say that no mischief and no harm were going on under far more difficult conditions of life than were encountered at home.[11]

Although he was referring to soldiers using the brothels, this statement could have been misinterpreted as referring to the WAAC.

It was at this difficult time for the Corps that Chalmers Watson resigned as Chief Controller. She wanted to spend more time with her family and look after her son, who was recovering from appendicitis. In her farewell order to the WAAC, Chalmers Watson stated that:

It is now a year since I took part in the initial conference held by the Secretary of State for War to establish a Women's Army. I did not then anticipate that I would be actively concerned in the development of this new organisation, which has importance both in the national interests at present, and for the position of women in the future. As the Corps is now well established and running, I feel it right to return to my home duties in Scotland, in accordance with the original arrangement made with the Military Authorities when I took office.[12]

However, there were those who believed that her resignation was directly related to the rumours of WAAC immorality. The newspapers drew no such conclusions, pointing out that Chalmers Watson had reached the end of her agreed twelve-month period with the Corps. They printed Chalmers Watson's denial that her resignation was due to the rumours, as well as her statement that "'[t]he persistence of these evil stories … makes me believe that there is an organised attempt, deliberately planned by enemy agents, to stop useful girls from joining the women's army.'"[13]

On 11 February 1918, Florence Leach was appointed as Chief Controller. The climate was such that she was asked to swear an affidavit stating that no member of the Corps had ever been requisitioned or sent to France for any immoral purpose whatsoever. Her first public engagement was at the Women's War Services Exhibition at Harrods, where she attended the opening and gave a lecture on a subsequent day.

The press published articles praising the WAAC, criticising their detractors and reporting on the continuing recruitment drive.

Commission of Enquiry

The authorities and the majority of the press were not able to successfully counteract the rumours through statements alone. On 11 February 1918, George Roberts appointed a Commission of Enquiry to travel to France. The aim was to carry out an independent enquiry into allegations of immoral conduct amongst the WAACs within the wider context of accommodation, discipline and supervision both at work and during recreation. The Commission was composed of five women. The Chair, Lucy Deane Streatfeild, had worked as a factory inspector and sat on a number of committees during the war, including the executive committee of the Women's Land Army in Kent. Violet Markham, Deputy Director of the Women's Section of the National Service Department, acted as the Commission Secretary. The remaining three women were Mary Carlin (Dock and General Workers' Union), Julia Varley (Workers' Union) and Muriel Ritson (Women's Friendly Society of Scotland).

George Roberts publically announced the appointment at the opening of the Women's War Service's Exhibition at Harrods. He was reported to have said that the rumours originated in pro-German quarters and that the Ministry meant:

> to scotch them, because they are part of a great scheme to demoralise the people of this country. Whenever we have evidence of persons circulating these rumours we shall at once take proceedings against them, and I venture to hope that where we do so these persons will not escape with a fine, but will be subjected to a severe term of imprisonment.[14]

The Commission visited France between 5 and 13 March 1918, accompanied by Florence Leach. Their arrival in France merited one line in Gwynne-Vaughan's War Diary. She rather begrudgingly facilitated their visit and went with them to a number of locations. They visited twenty-nine camps and three hospitals and interviewed the Chief Controller, as well as eighty other personnel including WAAC administrators, the AG, chaplains, base commandants and YWCA officials. When they met with the AG at GHQ, he drew their attention to the popular joke regarding a 'WAAC on the knee' and his expectation that they prevent such things.

Gwynne-Vaughan went into more detail in her War Diary on their departure, writing that their visit had not been good for discipline and it had been reported that some members of the Committee had questioned soldiers, passing along the road, about the behaviour of the WAAC.[15]

Dorothy Pickford met the Commission when they stayed at her camp for one night. She wrote in a letter home of the encounter and emphasised class distinction, both in terms of a member of the Committee and of the lower grades of the Corps:

> Julia Varley was the queerest little creature ... I believe she is quite a light in the Labour world? She began life in a Yorkshire factory, we know the type well but for the others she was something quite new. Social distinctions just did not exist for her, and I wish you could have heard her ordering tea and hot water when I took her to her room at night. Candidly I doubt very much if their visit will have any definite results. They addressed the workers on the necessity of correct deportment, but they, conscious in their own rectitude, are only furious that a word should be said against them. They have their standard of behaviour and very few transgress it, but it isn't always our standard.[16]

In March 1918, the Ministry of Information sent the journalist Fryniwyd Jesse to France. She spent time with the WAAC, as well as the VAD and the FANY. However, her resulting book – *The Sword of Deborah*[17] – was not published until shortly after the war. It included a chapter entitled *Waacs: Rumours and Realities,* in which she reported pregnancy statistics provided by the area controller (fifteen pregnant before arrival in France and five who became pregnant in France). She encouraged her readers to put these statistics into context, writing: '[c]ompare that with the morality of any village in England, or anywhere else in the world, and then say, if you dare to be so obviously dishonest, that there is any reason why the Women's Army should be aspersed.'[18]

Fryniwyd Jesse wrote very favourable accounts of the WAAC and their work in France.

Report Findings

The Commission's report was published on 20 March 1918. It concluded that '[a]s a result of our enquiry we can find no justification of any kind for the vague accusations of immoral conduct on a large scale which have been circulated about the WAAC.'[19] It went on to comment that:

> We feel that the large majority of the girls who have come forward in an hour of crisis and difficulty to share the work of the men in the field have upheld the honour of their sex and of their country in a spirit which should win for them the regard and gratitude of the nation.[20]

The Commission found that out of 6,023 women (the strength of the WAAC in France up to 12 March 1918), twenty-one had been reported as pregnant. Two of these women were married and most of the others were pregnant before arriving in France. There were twelve reported cases of venereal disease, of which two were doubtful and the others of old standing.[21]

The report considered the origin of the rumours. It drew attention to the differences between British and French society and suggested that the social mixing of the WAACs and soldiers may have at times been 'open to misconstruction.'[22] However, the Commission was keen to point out that this was the situation when the WAAC first arrived in France but that the situation had improved. They believed that the main origin of the rumours was in letters written by soldiers to their friends and family in the UK. The report was clear that there were men who disliked the WAAC because they themselves had been substituted by women. It set out other causes for such letters, for example idle rumour, but referred to these as 'probable.'[23] There is a sense that the authors were endeavouring to soften the drafting of a difficult message.

The Commission made a number of recommendations within the context of potentially increased numbers of WAACs serving overseas as the war progressed. They recommended that considerable care be taken when selecting future recruits at all levels, that powers of dismissal and transfer be used more regularly and that women police or patrols be instigated.[24]

The report was issued to the press on 14 April 1918 and was widely quoted the following day under jubilant headlines. It followed reports two weeks earlier of the bravery of the WAAC serving overseas during the Spring Offensive (see Chapter 6).

Society's View of the WAAC after the Report

The rumours, however, persisted, albeit it to a lesser degree. The War Office maintained a hard line in relation to prosecuting individuals accused of spreading rumours about the WAAC. On 15 April 1918, the Reverend Richard H. Quick, a Primitive Methodist Minister from Congleton, Cheshire, appeared in court charged under DORA with spreading false reports and making a false statement about the Corps. In a letter to the Secretary of the Purity League, he claimed that under a government order single pregnant women in the WAAC were given £15 and the child taken into the care of the authorities. The Reverend Quick argued that he had been making an enquiry as to whether such an order existed but was fined £40.

On 16 April 1918, William Henry Mainwaring, the local Secretary of the Unofficial Reform Committee of the South Wales Miners' Federation, appeared in court in Pontypridd, Wales, charged under DORA for spreading false reports at a public meeting in March 1918. He claimed that WAACs were being sent to brothels behind the lines in France. Florence Leach attended the court and stated that no member of the WAAC had been sent overseas for an improper purpose but to carry out specific work. William Mainwaring denied making the statements or referring specifically to the WAAC. He was sentenced to a £50 fine.

In May 1918, a new branch of the Corps was formed – a service of patrols – led by Controller of Patrols, Dora Esslemont. She had previously served with the Women's Patrols in connection with the London Police. The women who volunteered for the service from the WAAC were chosen on the basis of their good character and record of work. Their role was to work at camps and hostels to ensure discipline was maintained and that women kept within bounds and reported at the correct times. They wore a black brassard stamped with QMAAC in red lettering and carried a whistle on a white lanyard. They were also issued with a mackintosh and haversack.[25] The women trained at the WAAC camp in Bristol and their first patrols were in London from 1 August 1918. Their patrols at the camps in France began in September 1918 and they were initially accompanied by Dorothy Peto who had trained them. Dorothy Peto was the Director of the National Union of Women Workers (NUWW) Patrol Training School.

The Commission had observed in their report that the rumours had impacted negatively on the recruitment of women into the WAAC.[26] However, the numbers in the WAAC (at home and overseas) rose steadily from 20,198 in December 1917 to 33,026 in March 1918.[27]

In April 1918, approximately 1,000 women attended a recruitment meeting in Aberdeen. The attendance was so great that two meetings had to be held in different rooms. Interestingly, Muriel Ritson, who had been on the Commission of Enquiry, was at the meeting and spoke highly of the WAACs that she had observed in France. This was prior to the Commission's report being released to the press.

In June 1918, the National Service Department wrote to the War Office stating that rumours had reached them regarding the amount of liberty afforded to the WAAC in France. Further, they had received enquiries from parents who wanted to know the details of the hostel rules in France.[28]

In August 1918, there was yet another prosecution under DORA. Two women, Blanche Black and Murdine Gumbs, were fined at a court in Portsmouth for making statements likely to prejudice recruitment to the WAAC. Murdine Gumbs had said to two WAAC women that she would not lower herself to wear the uniform and that WAACs received £15 for each child.

Although the WAAC was exonerated and the rumours died down, a number of WAACs noted later that it impacted on their ability to find jobs after the war. Ruby Ord recalled that 'immediately after [the war] … one was occupied with trying to get a job. … It was very, very difficult if you'd been a WAAC because we weren't looked upon with favour by the people at home.'[29]

There is no evidence that the memory of the rumours impacted on recruitment to Women's Services prior to and at the beginning of the Second World War. History was to repeat itself when, in April 1942, a Committee was appointed to review the amenities and welfare conditions of the three Women's Services. The Chairwoman – Violet Markham – had served on the Commission of Enquiry in 1918. The Committee was appointed partly due to rumours regarding the conduct of service women, including claims of immorality and drunkenness. The Committee's report, published six months later, exonerated the women.

Chapter 6

Danger

Air Raids

From the time of their arrival in France in March 1917, the WAAC was subjected to air raids. The alarm, known as the maroon, would sound and the women would go to the designated shelter. The type of shelter differed, depending on the accommodation or place of work. There were, for example, sand bagged huts, open trenches and trenches with corrugated iron or wooden roofs, as well as sandbags. In Étaples, the women took cover with French civilians in nearby chalk caves, which were reputed to have been used by Napoleon to shelter his troops. The women accessed the caves on the other side of a field from the camp by walking through a trench covered by corrugated iron.

The raids took place both day and night. Mabel Peel recalled of the daytime raids that:

> these were far less nerve-wracking. Our airmen would go up to fight them, and we used to see the struggle in the air, the white wings of the planes glancing in the blue sky and little puffs of smoke all around them, for all the world like fluffy bits of cotton wool. Then the shrapnel would come clattering down and we would hastily take cover.[1]

The majority of women record in primary sources that they were not afraid during the raids. This may have been the case but it is difficult to know whether some did not want to admit to their fear. Clearly, there were others for whom the raids would have been a terrifying experience.

Gwynne-Vaughan often recounted the story of a unit of WAAC signallers during a particularly bad air raid on Boulogne. They remained at their posts at the French telephone exchange, which was located in a glass-roofed building. The officer in charge recommended to GHQ that they be mentioned in orders but GHQ responded that '[w]e do not thank soldiers for devotion to duty. We do not propose to treat these women differently.'[2] Gwynne-Vaughan appreciated this response as once again the Army treated the women in the same way as soldiers.

Damage was done to WAAC accommodation during the raids, including to huts in Calais. The WAAC camp at Étaples received direct hits and a number of huts in which the women slept, as well as the YWCA hut, were destroyed. Elsie Cooper wrote of the aftermath of the raid that:

> In the huts there was a little shelf where the walls joined the roof and we used to keep little things there. Our huts were supposed to be examined every day by the officers and we kept these well hidden – the tins of milk, we had a primus stove, a few eggs and lots of odds and ends which were kept up there. ... One early morning after a very bad raid we came back to the hut. We found everything from the shelves were all over the place, beds and floors. And the cat in the middle of the hut busy lapping up the milk, thoroughly enjoying it. Didn't know there'd been a raid on.[3]

The women would have been keen not to alarm family and friends at home. Elizabeth Johnston received a letter from her mother on 18 March 1918, who was concerned for her safety because, due to the censor, she had not received her daughter's expected communication. Elizabeth replied that:

> I can't tell you how sorry I am that you have been so worried. I nearly wept when I knew how anxious you have been. But, in future, never worry about me, please. You can always be perfectly sure

that if anything really serious happens, you will know immediately
… let me assure you, the chances of anything serious befalling a
W.A.A.C. are very remote indeed, in fact, nigh impossible.[4]

First German Offensive 1918

On 21 March 1918, the day after the Commission of Enquiry published
the report on the WAAC, the Germans launched the Michael Offensive
on the Somme. It was the first of four battles that made up the Spring
Offensive.

On 25 March 1918, the WAACs closest to the line of attack – cooks
and waitresses at Gézaincourt, near Doullens – were sent to Étaples.[5]
These women had catered for parties of visitors who required tours of
the Front. In terms of the Army, Army Schools were closed, forward
static units brought back and reinforcements brought in from camps
nearer to the coast. Consequently, many WAACs were redeployed
and found new accommodation. On 27 March 1918, WAACs from
the Third Army Infantry School in Auxi-le-Château were evacuated
by cattle truck to Abbeville and on to Boulogne.[6] On 28 March 1918,
the WAACs at Fourth Army Infantry School in Flixecourt moved to
Étaples and those at Fifth Army Musketry School in Pont Remy were
pulled back to the WAAC camp at Abbeville.[7]

After their own duties had been carried out, many WAACs were sent
to nearby military hospitals to assist, for example rolling bandages or
sitting with the men. Elizabeth Johnston, careful of censorship and her
parent's concerns, wrote home of the changes that were taking place as
a result of the offensive:

We have been asked if we are willing to give up our beds. "Signals"
gave them up right away; we are to be given wooden beds now,
about a foot from the floor. Also, a notice has been posted up asking
for the names of girls who are willing to devote their spare time
to hospital work. All our names are already down. So our days off
are booked now, and we are all looking forward to lending a hand
soon. I wouldn't be out of this for all the pearls of the South Seas.[8]

Charlotte Bottomley remembered the terrible reality:

> The ambulances were pouring in day and night. … We used to go
> in at night when we'd come off duty and light cigarettes when they
> were all lined up in stretchers waiting for medical attention and
> we were to go along giving them cigarettes and lighting them for
> them. Some of them were terribly bad. There was a bad gas attack.
> … A Canadian that I'd met … he came back badly gassed. I didn't
> know him. His neck and his shoulders were all in one … and he
> looked ghastly, he couldn't talk and that was with phosgene gas.[9]

She went to see him every day before they moved him to the UK. He
died on the sea journey home to Vancouver.

The WAACs based at Abbeville were now in the most forward
position and toward the end of March 1918 were on standby to evacuate.
Charlotte Bottomley spoke of the impact on the civilian population, as
well as on the WAAC:

> On the 25th of March there was trouble on in Amiens. It was
> being bombed and shelled incessantly and the civilian population
> were pouring into Abbeville, a most pathetic sight. Some with
> two-wheeled carts, some with barrows and others just carrying as
> much as they could manage to salvage from the onslaught – cattle
> and goats, hens and domestic pets. They passed by our camp in
> a never-ending procession, disappearing into the woods and on
> towards the coast. … We were instructed to keep a haversack at
> the ready with the minimum of toilet requisites and necessities,
> ready to beat a hasty retreat at a moment's notice. We stood firm
> and said we stood shoulder to shoulder with our men and if they
> stayed we did not retreat.[10]

On 30 March 1918, the women working with the AMTD in Abbeville
were moved to Calais and all WAACs without employment in Abbeville
were evacuated.

On 31 March 1918, Gwynne-Vaughan was called to GHQ and asked what would happen to the WAAC if the Germans advanced further. She presented a plan she had already prepared, which set out how the WAAC could be moved and accommodated in France. The plan was never executed, as the Army in France decided that they should remain attached to their offices. This was in complete contrast to the War Office, which wanted to remove the women to England.

The Germans called off the advance on 5 April 1918. The newspapers in the UK praised the WAACs for their behaviour in the face of adversity. They reported that the War Office had received accounts of the WAACs at an Army School who refused transport to a safer location. After the students had left, they remained and looked after men coming back from the line. The women then marched fifteen miles to a place of safety. This referred to the WAACs at Fourth Army Infantry School in Flixecourt and although they did provide food and drink to the men, they were driven the fifteen miles by truck. One phrase, which was credited to an official source, was published in a number of newspapers: 'The W.A.A.C. during the crisis have more than justified their existence, and have well maintained the credit of their sex and of the Army to which they belong.' There were also false reports of WAACs being captured by the Germans in the advance to Amiens. These were quickly refuted by the War Office. There were concerns that such rumours would have a negative impact on morale and recruitment.

Becoming the QMAAC

On 9 April 1918, the Secretary of State for War announced that:

As a mark of Her Majesty's appreciation of the good services rendered by the Women's Army Auxiliary Corps both at Home and Abroad since its inauguration, and especially of the distinction which it has earned in France by its work for the Army during the recent fighting on the Western Front, Her Majesty has been graciously pleased to assume the position and title of Commandant-in-Chief of the Corps, which in future will bear the name of Queen Mary's Army Auxiliary Corps.[11]

A special order was drafted two days later, which was to be read out loud to all members of the Corps. In it, the Chief Controller wrote that:

I feel sure that this will be a great incentive to each Member of the Corps to exercise every effort to reach the high standard of efficiency and good behaviour which it is our earnest endeavour to attain, and that it will be a still greater stimulus towards the feeling of esprit de corps which is the foundation on which an Army is built up.[12]

The WAAC officially became the QMAAC and a new cap badge was issued. However, the women continued to refer to themselves as WAAC.[13]

Queen Mary had visited the WAAC in Wimereux in July 1917 as part of a tour of the armies in France with her husband. The queen visited separate locations to those of the king, notably those further away from the Front. The War Diary for GHQ 1st Echelon for 8 July 1917 records how the WAACs lined the road as the queen's cavalcade drove by.[14] She had also attended the Women's War Services Exhibition at Harrods earlier in the year.

The queen took a very personal interest in the affairs of the Corps. In May 1918, she asked a number of written questions, which centred on the morality and welfare of the women. The questions included: what arrangements were made for WAACs on leave from France who found themselves alone in London at night; what instructions did administrators have in cases of grave moral conduct; and were young male cadets housed with the WAAC.[15]

Second German Offensive 1918

On the same day as the announcement regarding the QMAAC, the Germans launched the Georgette Offensive, also known as the Battle of the Lys.

The Ordnance Survey in Wardrecques near St Omer was close to the battles for Hazebrouk and Bailleul and was moved to Wimereux near Boulogne four days later. Some of the women in OBOS travelled to the UK before returning to France when their accommodation had been rebuilt. At the same time, Gwynne-Vaughan received orders that the 142 WAAC signallers at St Omer, whose behaviour had been excellent during the raids, were also to be evacuated, but this was overruled by the Director of Signals who regarded them as indispensable.[16]

The minority of WAACs remaining at Abbeville were the closest of the Corps to the fighting. Charlotte Bottomley and a colleague were kept on by the base commandant in Abbeville. She recalled that '[o]n April the 15th, Abbeville was put out of bounds except on duty. We weren't given a reason but we were on a nightly alert. And the guns certainly sounded nearer.'[17]

The second German offensive concluded on 29 April 1918.

Third German Offensive 1918

In May 1918, leaflets were dropped by the Germans on Abbeville warning that the town was going to be bombed, but the WAAC remained. On the night of 21 to 22 May 1918, Abbeville came under significant bombardment. Charlotte Bottomley had decided:

> to go down into the trenches and get settled before anything started. We got right to the end so that we didn't get trodden on. What a night. All hell let loose and the ammunition dump at Saigneville went up and lit the whole countryside up for miles around. Our Camp 2, on the Montreuil Road, got a whopper. But although the camp was destroyed no one was hurt apart from shell shock.[18]

Camp 2 had been hit by an aerial torpedo and four huts out of seventeen survived. The first photograph at plate five was taken the morning after the raid and shows the extent of the crater. The WAAC area controller visited the camp and issued clothing to members as uniforms and belongings had been blown across the camp, as well as trapped in the high branches of the trees. Gwynne-Vaughan and the Commander in Chief also visited the camp to see the damage for themselves. No women were killed but several received minor injuries as a result of the partial collapse of a trench in which they were sheltering. Unit Administrator Margaret Annabella Campbell Gibson received the Military Medal (MM) for her gallantry and devotion to duty during the raid. She was the first member of the Corps to receive the MM. Women in the WAAC were not able to be awarded the Military Cross as they did not hold commissions. Margaret Gibson did not survive the war. She died, aged 41, of dysentery on 17 September 1918 and is buried in Mont Huon Cemetery, Le Tréport, France.[19]

The raids continued at Abbeville a few days later. Charlotte Bottomley said that after yet another night in the trenches 'we had lost so much sleep and had to be at work during the day that spirits were at a low ebb and we were beginning to get aches and pains and feel off colour.'[20]

On the night of 29 to 30 May 1918, three aerial torpedoes were dropped on WAAC Camp 1 in Abbeville. One of the torpedoes made a direct hit on a covered trench in which women were sheltering. Eight women died at the scene and one was taken to No 2 Stationary Hospital but died of her injuries. Six women were injured. Dr Phoebe Chapple was at Camp 1 at the time of the raid and was able to assist with treatment. That night the women in Camp 1 were transferred to a YMCA hut at the ASC depot in Mautort. Area Controller Mary Frood visited the camp and the YMCA hut at 0230. The War Diary for Abbeville records the incident and the entry is short and to the point. Gwynne-Vaughan arrived at 0200 and described the incident in a little more detail in her own War Diary, commenting on the admirable behaviour of Mary Frood and Assistant Administrator Elizabeth

Sophy Cross. Later, in her autobiography, Gwynne-Vaughan recalled that one woman:

> disregarding shell-holes, had hurried in the dark for aid; a forewoman, though her shoes were blown off, worked unremittingly to rescue her comrades … . The area controller told me she had seen that a woman attending to the injured was limping. … A nail was embedded in [her foot] which she had been too busy to notice.[21]

On the morning of 30 May 1918, Gwynne-Vaughan went with Elizabeth Cross to No 2 Stationary Hospital, where the latter attempted to identify the deceased women.[22]

The nine WAACs were the first British women in the military to die on active service. They were:

Mary McLachlan Blaikley (Worker 31503). Aged 20 years and from Gartcosh in North Lanarkshire, Scotland.

Beatrice V. Campbell (Worker 31673). Aged 20 years and from Cupar in Fife, Scotland. She had previously worked in munitions and had been in France for six weeks.

Margaret Selina Caswell (Worker 15703). Aged 22 years and was born in Wiltshire, England.

Catherine Connor (Worker 34767). Aged 20 years and from Cambuslang in South Lanarkshire, Scotland. She had previously worked at the Singers' works in Clydebank and had been in France for several months.

Jeanie Grant (Worker 31918). Aged 22 years and from Airdrie in North Lanarkshire, Scotland.

Annie Elizabeth Moores (Worker 15695). Aged 27 years and born in Wiltshire, England.

Ethel Francis Mary Parker (Worker 9048). Aged 21 years. She had worked for the Precentor and his wife at Canterbury Cathedral in Kent, England.

Alice Thomasson (Worker 35588).

Jeanie H.L. Watson (Worker 34864). Aged 25 years and from Cambuslang in South Lanarkshire, Scotland, she had previously worked at the Cambuslang Dyeworks. Jeanie died in hospital later that night.[23] Two photographs of Jeanie, before and after enrolment in the WAAC, can be found at plates six and seven.

The women had been in France for a relatively short period. Many of the WAACs who had been in France for some time were upset that the honour of dying under fire had fallen to the new recruits. Indeed, Charlotte Bottomley recalled that '[t]hey were newly out from England and it annoyed us ... they hadn't been out long enough to be bombed and we'd been out all that time and got nothing.'[24]

The women were buried on 31 May 1918 in Abbeville Communal Extension Cemetery. They were given full military honours. Their coffins were carried on gun carriages from No 2 Stationary Hospital with members of the WAAC forming a cortège. The RAF flew overhead and soldiers, lining the route, saluted as the coffins passed by. Charlotte Bottomley was one of the WAACs who marched behind the coffins and found it to be a very moving experience: '[a]ll along the route soldiers stood to attention and civilians stood, many weeping.'[25] At the burial, soldiers fired a salute and the Last Post was sounded. Nora Barker was one of the WAAC gardeners who filled in the graves. She had been in the trenches in a camp on the other side of Abbeville on the night that the fatal attack occurred.

Some journalists initially misreported the incident as death by machine gun fire as the women crossed a field. On 31 May 1918, Gwynne-Vaughan recorded in her War Diary that she had had an interview with correspondents of *The Times* and other papers and had contradicted the story.[26] The press were once again supportive of the WAAC, but their articles were not sensational and the coverage of the incident was relatively small. The explanation for this can be found in Gwynne-Vaughan's autobiography. She explained that the morning after the bombing she was approached by journalists who wanted to condemn the Germans for killing women. However, Gwynne-Vaughan was clear that, as the WAACs were replacing men, the enemy was entitled to kill them if they could. She stated that '[t]he reporters saw the point and treated us most correctly, so that there was no fuss in the Press.'[27] One journalist quoted a WAAC officer as stating that:

> if we take the place of soldiers behind the lines we must take the risks that come in their way. We have been fortunate up to now. Not a single death has been reported in our corps. We mourn our comrades grievously, but we do not make any complaint. It is all in our day's work.[28]

Within a couple of days, eleven WAACs were sent back to the UK to be treated at the Endell Street Military Hospital, London. Some of them were physically injured and others were suffering from shell shock or what is now referred to as post-traumatic stress disorder (PTSD). One of the women was interviewed by a journalist and gave a first-hand account of the bombing:

> One of the machines had trouble with its engines, and came down within 20 ft of the ground, saw us, and released a bomb. It fell on the edge of the trench, dropping on to a loaded petrol lorry. The lorry blazed up, and revealed us all to the Huns, who then showered down bombs. ... I felt a piece of shrapnel in my side, but didn't say anything for fear of frightening the girl who was with

me, but she found her arm covered with blood, and instantly she seemed to lose all fear, and did what she could when I got a little faint.[29]

Queen Mary heard about these members of her Corps and arranged for those who were able to be moved to Queen Mary's Home for Governesses at Petersham Lodge in Richmond, Surrey.

Three WAACs received the MM for their actions on 30 May 1918: Assistant Administrator Elizabeth Cross, Forewoman Ethel Grace Cartledge and Dr Phoebe Chapple. Elizabeth Cross was knocked down but immediately got up and assisted Dr Chapple as the raid continued. Ethel Cartledge lost both her shoes and was wounded in one of her feet but she carried out her duties and kept the workers steady. It is likely that Ethel Cartledge is the forewoman referred to by Gwynne-Vaughan in her War Diary.

Prior to the fatal raid, a number of WAACs at Abbeville spent each night under canvas in nearby Crécy Forest. The forest had been where Edward the Third and the Black Prince had camped amongst the trees with their men before the defeat of the greater French Army in 1346. After the fatal raid at Camp 1, this precaution was extended to all WAACs at Abbeville. The WAAC camp in the forest was in close proximity to a German POW camp, which mitigated against the risk of enemy bombing. Each morning, the women were returned to Abbeville in lorries and brought back again in the evening. Eight women slept in each bell tent with their feet to the centre pole, but a number slept in the open or under a ground sheet suspended from poles. The second photograph at plate five shows WAACs sleeping in the open, wrapped in blankets and with tin hats at the ready. Charlotte Bottomley's future husband followed her out on one occasion on his motorbike and she described the experience of living in the forest in rather romantic tones: '[w]hat a lovely spell it was … . Wild strawberries in abundance, wild boars snorting in the distance and wild Canadians in the Forestry Corps, who were most anxious to fraternise but given orders to keep off.'[30] The conditions may have been more basic than in camp but it was summer and the women were at least in an area of relative safety. The lack of primary source material on this part of the WAAC's history means that it is difficult to assess how the women felt about the arrangement.

The fourth German offensive known as Gneisenau or the Battle of Matz commenced on 9 June 1918. On 13 June 1918, WAAC headquarters was transferred from Abbeville to St Valery-sur-Somme.

In July 1918, the number of WAACs in Abbeville had fallen to 351 and Camp 2 had been evacuated and handed back to the base commandant.[31] On 31 July 1918, it was considered safe for the WAACs at Abbeville to once again sleep at their camp and the camp in Crécy Forest was evacuated.

The Abbeville War Diary for this period details many workers being transferred to and from the WAAC rest camp at Mesnil-Val. This was established in the summer of 1918 to provide respite for women suffering from strain as a result of the Spring Offensive. The War Office would not sanction leave in addition to the allocated fortnight but did acknowledge that the women needed to rest. The WAACs ran the camp themselves, as well as guarding it.[32]

In August 1918 there was a direct hit on the deputy controller's office in Boulogne but there were no injuries or fatalities. By October 1918, new huts were being built at Camp 3 in Abbeville and the number of WAACs in the area increased to 460.[33]

The experience of the WAAC during the spring of 1918 demonstrated to the public at home the very real dangers that the women were exposed to. In total, thirty-nine WAACs were buried overseas between 1917 and 1920. Of these, nine died during bombing, seven of pneumonia, three of disease and one of accidental injuries. The cause of the remaining nineteen deaths is not known.[34]

The reports of attacks, both fatal and non-fatal did not have a negative impact on recruiting. As stated in Chapter 2, the number of new recruits remained high through the summer of 1918 in comparison with the same period in 1917.

On 1 September 1918, Gwynne-Vaughan was ordered to return to the War Office. She was informed that she had been appointed Commandant of the WRAF. She was not content with the decision but had no choice in the matter. Gwynne-Vaughan returned to France on 3 September 1918 to handover to her replacement – Lila Davy – who had been one of the original VAD superintendents at the Smoke Helmet Depot that transferred to the WAAC, and who later became the deputy controller at Rouen. Gwynne-Vaughan also addressed the women of the Corps directly, for example on 04 September 1918, she spoke to a parade of WAACs at Camps 1 and 3 in Abbeville.[35] She left France on 19 September 1918 and on that day Lila Davy's first job was to meet Dorothy Peto before she returned to the UK after escorting the first patrols to France.[36]

Chapter 7

Disbandment

Armistice

On 11 November 1918, Chief Controller Lila Davy recorded simply in her War Diary that, along with the usual office routine, news of the Armistice had arrived.[1] The majority of the WAACs in France were released from their duties and celebrated in different ways, for example attending a dance or going to watch processions in the towns. At GHQ 1st Echelon, there was a half-day holiday for all clerks who could be spared and a dance, to which the Army Ordnance Corps were invited, went on until midnight.[2]

In line with the rest of society, the WAACs variously described the Armistice as an anti-climax or a relief. Ruby Ord felt that the Armistice:

> was a bit anticlimax [sic] … all the people … you had known who were killed etc., they were just in the war zone, they could come home in your imagination. But the Armistice brought the realisation to you that they weren't coming back, that it was the end. And I think that it wasn't such a time of rejoicing as it might have been.[3]

Ruby did not go out of camp on Armistice Day, noting in her later interview that in France they were too near the reality of the war. Annie Martin considered that the Armistice was a great relief:

> because by this time we'd all lost so many of our young men – brothers, cousins, friends. It was a great relief to know that the

war was over ... and it was a great relief ... to know that we should go through the night without an air raid.[4]

One of Annie Martin's brothers was killed two weeks before the Armistice.

Elizabeth Johnston wrote an article about the Armistice that was published in the *East of Fife Observer*. She had worked during the night before the Armistice and with her fellow signallers went into Rouen on 11 November 1918. She wrote:

> we decided to leave the town, and await the news on the hill-top; we knew what the signal was to be, and how the signing of the Armistice was to be proclaimed. When we reached the summit of the hill, we came on a party of German prisoners burying a dead comrade. How significant it seemed! ... Suddenly, the hillside echoed and re-echoed, as volley after volley was fired from the big gun on the ramparts. In the distance, the cathedral bells pealed and clanged out the good news.[5]

She and her friends finished the night at the British cemetery near their camp, where they laid flowers amongst the graves of soldiers, nurses and WAACs.

On 20 November 1918, Princess Mary travelled to France to visit women war workers. It was her first independent state visit and she was the first Royal to go to France after the Armistice. She was met, among others, by Chief Controller Lila Davy who offered her female driver to lead the cavalcade. This was refused by the Assistant Provost Marshall and the procession subsequently became lost. When the Princess said good night to the WAAC driver on their return, the girl informed the Princess that 'the halt on the road on the way out was the result of trusting to the care of a mere man rather than to a member of the Q.M.A.A.C.'s! The Princess was much amused at this earnest explanation.'[6]

On the second day of her visit, the Princess visited Abbeville, where she saw the crater left by the bomb during the fatal air raid. She also visited the WAAC convalescent home at Étretat, the bakery in Dieppe – where she took tea – and the WAAC drivers' camp and telephone exchange at Rouen. Elizabeth Johnston, who worked in the latter, wrote home of the concert which the WAAC put on in her honour:

> She ... is perfectly lovely, and so natural; a girl first, and then a Princess. She seemed to enjoy the concert immensely. The Signal girls sang verses and chorus composed by me, funny bits, all pertaining to the W.A.A.C.s, etc. She did laugh. If you could have seen her clapping her hands, and convulsed with laughter! She was in a V.A.D. uniform, with a close-fitting cap and looked lovely. ... She shook hands so heartily with the Administrators, who were presented to her, and chatted so naturally.[7]

The concert was attended by 650 WAACs, representing every unit and selected on the basis of their long service and good conduct. At the end of the concert, Lila Davy asked the Princess to take back to Queen Mary a message of loyalty and affection from the Corps. The Princess agreed in what was her first public speech and was met with applause, cheers and a short rendition of 'For She's a Jolly Good Fellow.'

In Boulogne, before her return home, the Princess was taken to see the women of the Ordnance Survey who were engaged in making maps of Germany. She also visited the camouflage factory staffed by French women and overseen by a WAAC administrator. They put on a demonstration that included asking the Princess to walk on duckboards during which a potential 'sniper' disguised beneath grass and vegetation was revealed.

Work and Recreation

The WAAC continued to work in France and occupied Germany for three reasons. First, the Armistice did not guarantee peace, as any deviation from the terms of the Armistice would have resulted in renewed hostilities. Second, it would take considerable time and resource to dismantle and remove the machinery of war. Third, the emphasis was on the men and facilitation of their return to civilian life. In the same way that, in 1917, the WAACs had been recruited to free men to fight, they were continuing to be enrolled until the beginning of 1919 so that men could be demobilised.

The Corps was assigned a number of new duties, for example border control. As a result of food being sent to France and occupied Germany, smuggling routes opened up into unoccupied Germany. The WAACs worked on trains and trams, carrying out searches of civilian women at the last stops and stations before reaching unoccupied Germany. The WAACs also checked passports at Cologne Station.

Charlotte Bottomley remembered the poignancy of one of her roles after the Armistice. Each day she had to phone the hospitals to find out how many men had died, arrange for coffins to be made and General Service wagons to collect the bodies. She noted that '[i]t was sad that boys should still go on dying, even when the battle was over. I remember thinking about it.'[8]

A detachment of clerks and domestic workers was also attached to Headquarters, Director of Graves Registration and Enquiries based at St Pol. It was at the chapel at St Pol, on the night of 7 November 1920, where the bodies of the four unknown soldiers lay prior to being taken to Boulogne the following day. Later, in 1946, Vere Maunsell-Thomas (née Brodie), the former unit administrator, recalled that:

We of St Pol can never forget the simple dignity in which the representative of all of the British nation who had laid down their lives came to existence in our camp chapel, and the proud sorrow that we felt.[9]

The women continued to work long hours but there were more opportunities for dances, concerts, entertainments and taking part in sports. They were also able to travel further afield on sightseeing excursions. Shortly after the Armistice, the WAAC went on tours of the battlefields. The War Diary for GHQ 2nd Echelon records one worker departing on Christmas Day 1918 for such a tour.[10] Emily Rumbold described seeing the ruins of the Cloth Hall in Ypres, as well as finding the grave of Prince Maurice of Battenburg marked by a little white cross on the outskirts of the town. On visiting Passchendaele Ridge, she remarked on the devastation there that '[h]owever any man came out alive I can't think.'[11] She noted the difference between the Allied trenches and those of the Germans which were dug deeper and had electric light. She recalled that she and her friends took their picnic lunch and sat on the ground with their feet in a shell hole.

As time passed, many women used their leave to travel further distances, for example into Brussels and Germany, where they went as far as Berlin. They travelled by 'lorry jumping', whereby they obtained lifts from army lorries.

Influenza

Between the summers of 1918 and 1919, a second wave of influenza ravaged France. The sick rate for WAAC attached to the AEF was high, with ten per cent off duty at one stage in February 1919. Emily Rumbold was in Vendreux at the time and recalled that the strongest men seemed to die quickly. Her colonel called her to the office to tell her that he was to be taken to hospital and the staff sergeant had the WAAC office disinfected. She knew one woman who died of the illness.[12]

Elizabeth Johnston fell ill with influenza at the beginning of December 1918. She wrote home from hospital but did not reference any deaths from influenza until she had been discharged from No 8 Stationary Hospital and returned to Camp 4 at Quevilly:

The 'flu cases kept coming in every day, and quite a number of the girls have been sent to Blighty. The Signal girl, who died, had a terrible struggle, she was so awfully ill. After a bit, they pumped oxygen into her lungs three times a day. Her people were sent for, but her sister didn't arrive until the day after she died. She was given a military funeral. Signal men carried her, and nearly all the Signal girls and officers were there.[13]

Mutiny

At this time, there was mutiny by men at some camps because of the method of demobilisation. Men who were in the lines of communication wanted to be demobilised in turn with those coming back from the front line. Further, men who had key roles back in the UK were returned first, which meant that many men who had been called up last went back before those who were called up before them. The WAACs continued to work during the mutinies despite the threat of eviction from their places of work by the men. Emily Rumbold worked next to an Army Ordnance camp in Calais. The men went on strike but the women went down to the depot as usual. Their major told them to stay away as there were 100 men marching down ready to throw out the girls who were working. Subsequently, a general was sent down from the line to deal with the mutiny. He consented to receive a deputation of men and after agreeing to look into their concerns, gave them two days to get back to work or they would be fired on. She recalled that they were all restricted to camp and 'had machine gunners in our office and they didn't leave until we ... were all working again.'[14]

Suspicious Death and Murder

On 13 June 1919, the body of a WAAC worker, Annie Winifred Mary Smith, was washed ashore at Dieppe. She was 25 years old and worked at the bakery. On that day, her parents had written to her giving their consent to marriage to a soldier who was originally from the UK but had emigrated to Canada and returned with a Canadian regiment. The unit administrator wrote to her parents of the death and the probability that she had fallen from a cliff. On the same day, they also received a letter from WAAC headquarters in London, stating that Annie had died at No 5 Stationary Hospital of a gunshot wound. The War Office was unable to provide any further details and her parents subsequently travelled from Flitwick, Bedfordshire to France to try and find out what had happened to their daughter. It was confirmed that she had been shot.

Annie, who was known as Winnie, was buried with full military honours at Janval Cemetery, Dieppe. In the following days and weeks, the story was widely reported in the British press as a mystery. Her sister stated that she had joined the WAAC after the death of her brother at the Battle of Loos. The family did not believe that she had committed suicide and spoke highly of her fiancé – Staff Sergeant Yeatman – who they had come to know a little through his letters to Annie's father, as well as Annie's description of him.

Two days after Annie's body was found, Yeatman's body was washed up on the shore in Dieppe. He had a gunshot wound inflicted by the same gun that had killed Annie. The gun was a German revolver.

While her parents were in France, the sister received a letter from a friend of Annie who claimed that Annie had been 'wickedly deceived' by her fiancé, but would say no more, other than that she would be on leave in the UK in July and would discuss the matter further then. In the meantime, the papers reported that the Chaplain had questioned Yeatman about his marital status, believing him still married rather than a widower. On the day before the wedding was to have taken place, the Canadian had been informed the marriage could not be solemnised. The couple were seen that afternoon heading towards the cliffs. The truth of the matter i.e. if it was a double murder, a murder and suicide, or a joint suicide, will never be known.

The death of Annie came a month after the murder of another WAAC, Nellie Rault, at Haynes Park Camp in Bedfordshire. Nellie, originally from Jersey, had been in the Women's Legion and joined the WAAC in 1917 as a cook. A search was instigated after she missed roll call one morning, but her body was not found until two days later. She had been stabbed a number of times and her body hidden in the woods not far from the camp gates. A company sergeant major in the Royal

Engineers, who had been out with Nellie a number of times including the night before she disappeared, was arrested and charged. He was later discharged and the case was never solved.

Peace Treaty and Demobilisation

The War Office published the *Report of the Women War Workers Resettlement Committee* on 18 November 1918.[15] The objective of the report was to consider the arrangements for re-settling women under the control of the War Office back into civilian life. Florence Leach and Gwynne-Vaughan were both on the report committee. The report explained that it was not possible to provide definite recommendations due to the complexity of the problem. This included the fact that the government policy regarding the retention of organisations, including the WAAC, was unknown. Further, it was not possible to forecast how many women would want to stay in similar employment or move to other employment. The report set out a scheme of demobilisation based on the provisional scheme that had been worked out for the WAAC. In summary, the women would be issued with a dispersal certificate and medically examined to check fitness for travel. Officials would return to WAAC headquarters in the UK and members to the dispersal hostel in Folkestone. It was recommended that all receive twenty-eight days furlough on full pay and a railway warrant home. They would be allowed to wear their uniform during the twenty-eight days and only afterwards by sanction of the War Office.

The proposed criteria by which women would be selected for demobilisation were laid down in the report. The emphasis was on the home. Married women and widows with children would be released first, followed by single women who had a firm offer of employment or were qualified to undertake work in areas for which there was significant demand. This meant that length of service was not the determining factor. The key principle was that the women, including those in the WAAC, would be demobilised when they could be spared and not, as in the case of soldiers, as soon as possible.

The Treasury, however, was keen that the War Office arrange for the early demobilisation of the WAAC as it wanted simply to save money. In February 1919, the War Office wrote to the Treasury advising that not only had many women been retained as they would have been replaced by men, more had been enrolled in order to demobilise men or WAACs who had served twelve months. The new WAAC recruits were enrolled for only twelve months.[16] A note on the front of the file reveals the frustration felt by the Treasury:

> I find it hard to understand what work these women are doing but for the present I fear there is no further action that we can take. … Let us hope that there will be no "Army of Occup." bonus for these ladies![17]

At the end of March 1919, the War Office announced that the Army Council had decided that the WAAC would be maintained as part of the post-war army organisation.

On 28 June 1919 the Peace Treaty was signed and on 14 July 1919 many of the WAAC joined the Peace Parade in Paris. Additionally, a number were sent to the UK for the parade in London five days later. Emily Rumbold was one of these women and believed it was because she was a certain height. Her main concern was the uniform that she was required to wear:

> When we found we had to wear issue shoes and issue frocks twelve inches from the ground … no we couldn't possibly march through London with frocks twelve inches from the ground and issue shoes because we were allowed to buy our own you see.[18]

After the signing of the Peace Treaty, the Corps began to close down units in France, but the women remained overseas to fill gaps left by men who were being demobilised. Some WAACs were returned home on compassionate grounds, but approximately 8,000 WAACs remained in France.

In September 1919, the WAAC headquarters moved to Boulogne and later to nearby Wimereux, where it closed on 31 October 1919.

At this time, some sections of the press asked why the WAAC was still employed and stated that it was a financial burden. A female correspondent writing for *The Times* questioned the type of work that the women carried out and asked whether there was still room in the Army for domestics when there was a shortage in civilian life. The journalist acknowledged that the Women's Services needed time to tidy their affairs but stated that:

> They have done good work, and have earned full recognition and appreciation. To be frank, the public has grown tired of uniformed women. A year ago they could not do enough for them. Now they don't like them a bit, and are not making things too pleasant. The Army in Peace has no place for women.[19]

Questions were also asked about how the women spent their time in France, the inference being that they were engaged in recreation rather than useful employment. In late September 1919, the WAACs in France protested to Whitehall about such claims in the press and as a result, the War Office requested a report on the numbers of women remaining in France and detail as to how they were occupied.

The Army announced the payment of a bonus backdated to 1 May 1919, to women in the WAAC who undertook a new engagement to serve until 30 April 1920 or had already undertaken to serve for a longer period.

On 11 November 1918 there were 1,077 officials and 39,915 members in the WAAC both at home and in France. By July 1919, there were 721 officials and 19,296 members at home and in France.[20]

In September 1919, demobilisation of the WAAC was accelerated and on 21 September 1919, the first draft of WAACs to be demobilised in France reached Folkestone. In the following months, the WAACs were dispersed at a rate of 200 per day and replaced by male army recruits.

In December 1919, the War Office announced that the WAAC would cease to exist as an organised body at the end of that month. By 31 December 1919, all WAACs in France had returned to the UK for demobilisation. The exception was WAACs in the unit working at St Pol who had accepted the bonus to continue their work. The unit reported directly to the War Office.

The Chief Controller wrote an order to the women in which she placed her appreciation on record. She looked to a future in which the WAAC would continue to contribute to society, writing that:

> It is beyond question that the honour of the Corps will be upheld by all ranks on their return to civil life. It is hoped that the spirit of good comradeship, cheerfulness and courage in the face of discomforts and difficulties, which has bound the Corps together during the war, will continue to work for the public good, during the difficult period of reconstruction, which the British Empire has now entered upon.[21]

On 16 January 1920, the Army Council expressed their appreciation of the WAAC in Army Council Order 5, which was reported in the newspapers. The order stated that:

> The assistance rendered by the officials and members of the corps, who came forward so willingly at a time of grave crisis, has earned the gratitude and won the admiration, not only of the Army, but of the whole nation. Difficulties, discomfort, and, in many cases, the dangers of war have always been faced bravely and cheerfully, and the discipline of the corps throughout is worthy of the highest praise, and has been in accordance with the best traditions of the Army.[22]

The newspapers once again published articles that praised the Corps and thanked them on behalf of the public for their service.

On 30 April 1920 the WAAC finally ceased to exist and Controller in Chief Florence Leach was relinquished of her duties. She continued to work as the President of the QMAAC OCA.

The unit at St Pol kept in touch with ex-WAACs through letters to the OCA Gazette. At Christmas 1920, they wrote that:

> We who are still serving appreciate more than can be expressed any remembrance from our sister ex-Waacs. … We are just a little prouder of the whole corps, and we know we must keep up the reputation of the past members just as much as our own. The old Waacs thoughts of us do therefore help a good deal, and please give every reader of the Gazette the love and best wishes of their little unit of comrades still serving.[23]

The thirty-one women, led by Unit Administrator Vere Brodie, finally left France on 26 September 1921. Vere Brodie wrote a letter to the OCA Gazette that described their journey home.[24] She described how when they marched out of the camp with the men, the French watched them as they passed by and shouted out their farewells. At Calais, they separated from the men who would leave two days later – the last to leave France. The WAACs were waved off by a crowd at the quay and Vere Brodie wrote that '[i]t was really "the last Waacs leaving France," and, though it was sad, it was also wonderful. The end of a corps that had counted.'[25] They missed their train at Dover and therefore the welcoming party at Victoria Station made up of Florence Leach and members of the OCA, as well as the press. Florence Leach did go out later to meet them when they finally arrived. They were demobilised at the War Office on 27 September 1921, where they received their dispersal certificate and a railway warrant for their journey home. This was followed by a visit to the Command Paymaster. The following day a number of the women laid a wreath at the Cenotaph and visited the Tomb of the Unknown Soldier, whose remains had lain in the chapel at St Pol the previous year.

Four women in the unit from St Pol were able to claim the longest service record in the WAAC as they had been amongst the first to join in 1917: 420, Forewoman M. Griffiths (joined 9 May 1917); 465, Forewoman M. McWilliam, (joined 15 May 1917); 470, Worker N. O'Connor (joined 13 May 1917); and 182, Worker E. Norden (joined 28 April 1917), who had demobilised from St Pol on 03 March 1921.[26]

Although officially demobilised, a number of ex-WAACs remained working with the Army in Cologne, including at the Ordnance Base Depot and Officers Clothing Depot.[27] Many of these were civilian clerks who had arrived after the Armistice and were enrolled in the WAAC.

Each woman's view of their experience in the WAAC was dependent on their individual circumstances. For example, Annie Martin felt the war had not changed her: 'I did the work I'd been accustomed to doing. The living conditions were quite different but one returned to normal. It seemed as though one had only been away.'[28] She also believed that the sacrifices made during the war were worth it. In contrast, Ruby Ord did think that war had changed her because '[i]t was such an unusual experience for our day to go away from home and to be with so many other people, living always amongst a crowd. It was very good for one.'[29] She did not feel that the sacrifices were worth it and became a pacifist after the war.

An ex-WAAC wrote to the OCA with her emotional response to leaving the Corps and the adjustment to civilian life in peacetime:

I am proud to have belonged to the dear old corps, and only wish it were still in existence. The life was so open, free, and healthy, and a much more natural one than that which our return to civil life offers. ... Conditions were not always of the rosiest, but as I look back I feel certain that the very happiest years of my life were spent there [Abbeville]. The glorious comradeship, the feeling that we were really up against things, and doing something that was really worthwhile, fired us with enthusiasm and interest, and gave us something to hold on to, that was true and real, and brought to the surface the highest and best ideals. We were able to know and understand one another much better than we can ever hope to do under the conditions of ordinary life. These days of peace that we have looked forward to, and prayed for so long, seem to fall very short of expectations. I suppose things have hardly had time to shake down into their proper course. The dislocation after so many years of warfare must of course require careful nursing, and healing time.[30]

Society's View of the WAAC after the Armistice

In 1918 and before the Armistice, Ethel Tweedie wrote that:

Today every man is a soldier, and every woman is a man. Well, no – not quite; but, speaking roughly, war has turned the world upside down; and the upshot of the topsy-turvydom is that the world has discovered women, and women have found themselves. And a new world has been created.[31]

This view is in contrast to the fact that on 11 November 1918, the front page of the *Daily Mirror* announced that the women war worker's beauty competition was still open and that women who had served in France, including WAACs, should submit their photograph.[32]

The primary sources portray a mainly positive view held by ex-WAACs of their service during the war, but negative comments are made about their situation immediately after demobilisation and return to civilian life. Annie Martin was keen to inform her interviewer in the 1970s of the attitude of the British people:

which was not good. For instance in 1919 we had a reunion … and we went to a … guesthouse … . The first night at supper … I sat next to a lady. She turned to me with a face of horror and she said "Do you know there are some ex-WAACs in this house?" So I said "Yes, I happen to be one of them … and the person on your right next to you is another." I don't know what she expected to see but she was so horrified … . That is indicative of the way in which the general British public viewed us at the time.[33]

Ruby Ord complained of the way that they were viewed as the women who followed the men to France.[34] This suggests that the prejudices directed against the WAAC since its inception had not been removed either by the Commission's Report of March 1918 or positive press stories about their exemplary behaviour during the Spring Offensive.

Ruby Ord also explained that this affected their ability to get work after the war:

we weren't looked upon with favour by the people at home. We had done something that was outrageous for women to do, we'd gone to France etc. and left our homes and all that sort of thing. We had quite a job getting fixed up.[35]

Finding Work

It was difficult for many of the WAACs to find a new role for themselves immediately after the war. This was not solely because of the negative view of ex-WAACs in some quarters. Society wanted women who had taken on men's work or war work for the duration to return to their previous gendered roles. There was an emphasis on returning to the home to re-establish family life or to have more children. This was acceptable to many women, but there were others who wanted to remain in the work force but not return to the types of employment that they were in prior to the war, particularly domestic service. This was contrary to social expectation for two reasons.

First, women were expected to return to domestic service as not only was there a national shortage, but also this was considered to be a feminine role. In December 1918, the *Daily Mirror* reported that women who had undertaken war work were refusing to return to domestic service. It also quoted Miss Franklin, Secretary of the Women's Industrial Council who stated that:

There will be … plenty of good servants when the W.A.A.C.s are released … but hardly one will take a place in the old way. They are now used to working hard during definite hours, and being allowed to play as hard during an equally definitive free time.[36]

Ex-WAACs were singled out as being well suited to this work category because of their training. A number of former WAACs did join the Women's Legion Household Service Section. The newspapers contained advertisements for domestic staff, which explicitly requested applications from ex-WAACs. However, many were not keen to take up these offers of employment. In January 1919, the Treasury noted the shortage of domestic servants and was concerned that the out-of-work donation scheme would result in discharged WAACs, who were formally domestic servants, not returning to their previous occupations.[37] In 1919, the government stopped out-of-work donation payments for ex-domestic servants who refused to return to their former category of employment.

Second, it was a time of increased unemployment and men were given precedence over women. Women who had worked in industry were moved out immediately the war was over so that returning soldiers could return to civilian employment. WAACs who wanted to work after the war had to compete with the thousands of women who had lost their civilian war work. The *Report of the Women War Workers Resettlement Committee* recommended that women who had worked under the War Office should be specifically included within the Ministry of Labour machinery. For example, that the women should complete Civil Employment forms on cessation of hostilities to be submitted in bulk to the ministry, and individuals subsequently contacted directly and provided assistance to find work.

In July 1920, the QMAAC OCA reported that:

It is satisfactory to be able to record that after a somewhat disheartening experience at first the great majority of ex-Q.M.A.A.C. are now settled in civilian employment. Efforts have been made to give them all the help possible by putting them in touch with the various agencies likely to be of use, and by private inquiries. A number have been helped by the Central Committee for Women's Training, by Women's Service, by the Central Bureau, by the Employment Exchanges, and by the Professional Women's Registry. Several have shown great enterprise in starting schemes of their own, and we hope to be kept informed of their progress.[38]

It went on to state that the demand for women's labour was in teaching, nursing and domestic work. In terms of their own schemes, ex-WAACs established, for example, residential clubs, tea rooms and hire car companies.

The senior officials went on to occupy key positions in a variety of occupations, for example, Chalmers Watson became Chairwoman of the Board for *Time and Tide* magazine, Gwynne-Vaughan returned to Birkbeck as the head of the Botany Department and Hilda Horniblow ran a training centre for demobilised women.

At least one ex-WAAC who served in France is known to have committed suicide faced with an uncertain future.[39]

Emigration

In June 1918, at a conference of the Joint Council of Women's Emigration Societies, a female speaker stated that she had met WAACs who wanted to emigrate after the war. She claimed that they were enamoured of the soldiers from the colonies and did not want to return to domestic service in the UK.

In November 1918, the Resettlement Committee was aware that emigration may have been an option on demobilisation but believed that it was likely to be a year after demobilisation before a considerable programme could take place.

From April 1919 the Government Oversea[40] Settlement Committee ran a scheme whereby ex-service men and women, who had served a minimum of six months, could apply for free passage to other Commonwealth countries. For ex-service women, the scheme was scheduled to run until 31 December 1920. Former WAACs were dealt with by the Women's Section of the Oversea Settlement Committee. Any women from other Commonwealth countries who had served in the WAAC were repatriated at no expense to themselves.[41]

Female commissioners were appointed to visit Canada, Australia and New Zealand to ascertain what employment opportunities were available to ex-service women. The vacancies were mainly as agricultural or domestic workers, but the requirement was greater for the latter. In December 1919, the War Office advised WAAC headquarters that applicants willing to undertake domestic service were more likely to be successful and that this should be explained to any woman who answered 'no' to this category on their form.[42] Emigration was not necessarily the solution many ex-WAACs were hoping for, but it did provide them with the opportunity for adventure.

In addition, in August 1919, the Committee informed Florence Leach that £250,000 had been allocated to the WAAC, which would be doubled if deemed necessary.[43] The funds were to assist individuals who were not entitled to passage under the government scheme but who had suffered directly as a result of the war.

Ex-WAACs required the recommendation of WAAC headquarters as part of their application for the Oversea Settlement Scheme. As a result, the WAAC had oversight of the application process of its members and the War Office maintained a central record of applications. The women were asked a range of questions, including whether: they intended to work on the land or (in the case of women) in domestic service and if not in what profession; they had definite employment on arrival; they had dependents; and had friends or relatives in the country. The Corps was also requested to include any remarks relating to the woman and her reasons for emigration. Applicants were interviewed by a representative of the country of destination. Florence Leach was involved in direct communication with the Oversea Settlement Committee to ensure that ex-members of the WAAC were furnished with sufficient information to make a decision. She also represented women who had specific queries or requests, for example those who had married Commonwealth soldiers and wanted to travel back with them or who wished to be repatriated to their own country.

Women who emigrated at their own expense but who were subsequently successful in their application to the Oversea Settlement Committee were entitled to a refund (calculated at Third Class rate).

The Society for Overseas Settlement of British Women (SOSBW) and the Colonial Intelligence League regularly supplied WAAC headquarters with details of vacancies. A firm offer of employment would facilitate a woman's application for free passage.

In September 1920, the OCA reported that relatively few women had emigrated, citing the example of New South Wales to which thirty women a month had been sent, totalling 250, when they could process 100 a month.[44] In December 1920, the OCA published the overall statistics relating to the emigration of ex-service women: 687 in total of which 334 had gone to Canada, 210 to Australia and New Zealand, eighty-five to Africa, fifteen to India and the remainder to New Guinea, Ceylon, West Indies, Hong Kong, Egypt, Malay States and Straits Settlements.[45] The scheme was extended until 31 December 1921. The OCA Gazette published details of overseas vacancies supplied to them by SOSBW, as well as private individuals. It also published letters from ex-WAACs who had emigrated. These letters were for the most part positive, but a number did warn that any woman contemplating following them needed to be aware that conditions could be difficult. By 31 December 1921, over 1,000 ex-WAACs had emigrated under the Oversea Settlement Scheme.[46]

Although the Oversea Settlement Scheme had come to an end, women were still required overseas, particularly in domestic roles. The SOSBW continued to assist ex-service women, including ex-WAACs into the 1930s.

Financial Terms on Discharge

At the beginning of December 1918, the War Office wrote to the Treasury setting out its proposals for the terms to be given on discharge from the WAAC and other enrolled Corps. The War Office was concerned that women who had served overseas should not return with just the balance of their last week's pay. They proposed twenty-eight days furlough on full pay. Further, that mobile members (not officials) enrolled for the duration receive military out-of-work donation payments.[47] A note in the file by a Treasury official reveals that they considered the proposals as concessions as the terms, although not included in the contract, would not have been refused in better economic times. The Treasury believed that the War Departments were not keen on the proposals, but were being encouraged by the Ministry of Labour's concerns regarding a public outcry if the proposals were refused 'representing that popular opinion regards the Women's Corps as soldiers and entitled to soldiers' benefits'.[48] In the same month, the Treasury agreed to give two months pay to officials on discharge on the condition that they were not eligible for out-of-work donation payments and that mobile members would receive fourteen days furlough on full pay. WAACs enrolled after the Armistice were not entitled to benefits on discharge. Demobilisation benefit was not payable to the family of WAACs who died in service after 11 November 1918.

In January 1919, Sir Charles Harris, the Assistant Financial Secretary to the War Office, challenged the Treasury decision in a private memo. He had spoken to the female heads of the WAAC, WRNS and WRAF who anticipated a demonstration in Whitehall. He was keen to point out that it was often difficult to predict when their services would no longer be required and they were usually given the month's wages in lieu of notice that they were contractually entitled to. This would be complicated if women who were given warning of their discharge received only fourteen days on full pay. Further, he reminded the Treasury that many of the women had served under fire and been involved in the Spring Offensive.[49] The War Office subsequently wrote to the Treasury to say that they could not accept the decision regarding pay to mobile members on discharge, stating that soldiers and the public regarded the WAAC as women-soldiers and therefore entitled to similar benefits.[50] The Treasury agreed to twenty-eight days furlough for mobile members with a view to facilitating the speedy demobilisation of the WAAC.

Compensation

After the war, a number of local War Pensions Committees made strongly worded representations to their Association that ex-service women should be treated equally in terms of compensation for sickness or injury experienced directly as a result of their war service, both at home and overseas. They were not entitled to a pension, although women who served in the Women's Services overseas were entitled to compensation under the Injuries in War (Compensation) Act 1914, but the cases of some ex-service women, including WAACs, had either been refused or they were not content with the amount of compensation. One example submitted by a local War Pensions Committee was that of a clerk who served in France and after a few months was admitted to hospital with nervous debility and gastric ulcers. She was discharged as medically unfit and, unable to work and with no parents, was reliant on a family member. She received no compensation.[51] In addition, the War Office Medical Boards were considered to be inconsistent in their approach, women were discharged from hospital before their treatment was complete and many women with little formal education found it difficult to pursue their claim without assistance. At the end of November 1918, the Ministry of Pensions and the War Office planned to hold a conference to discuss the situation and shortly afterwards the matter became more pressing. On 4 December 1919, Captain Loseby MP (Bradford East) asked a question in the House of Commons regarding the equal treatment between ex-service women and men who had served overseas in terms of disability pensions and suggested that an inquiry take place.[52]

A meeting was subsequently held on 12 December 1919 between the Ministry of Pensions, representatives of the WAAC, WRNS and WRAF, as well as the Treasury, to draft a response to Captain Loseby's question. The Ministry of Pensions was opposed to bringing the women under the Pensions Royal Warrant because the women were enrolled, not enlisted, in the Services on a voluntary basis and it would set a precedent for other categories of person, for example workmen employed by contractors in war areas.[53] It was considered that part of the problem lay in the fact that WAACs, when demobilised or discharged, were not informed by the Service Departments of their right to claim compensation in certain circumstances. The answer to Captain Loseby's question, which had been postponed so that the Ministry of Pensions could meet with all three Services, was heard in the House of Commons on 19 February 1920.[54] There would be no enquiry but the War Office issued new instructions, which explained the women's rights more clearly. The Captain's response was to ask again why a woman was not to be treated in the same way as a man. A subsequent letter from the Ministry of Pensions to the Treasury reveals concerns that the Prime Minister's reply did not go far enough and that local War Pensions Committees were likely to continue to press the matter.[55] Indeed, Captain Loseby and Viscount Curzon MP (Battersea South) once again raised the question of equality in the House on 26 February 1920 and 4 March 1920. They were not satisfied that a woman in the Services overseas who might lose a limb in shell fire was not treated in the same way as a soldier or a private in the Labour Corps.[56] On 4 March 1920, details of the conditions for compensation to ex-service women, which remained unchanged, were published in the press.

The following day, the Ministry of Pensions hosted a conference attended by the Treasury, the War Office and representatives of the Women's Services. The WAAC was represented by Florence Leach and Edith Thompson. It was noted that it was difficult to directly attribute illness, rather than injury, to service. Those cases for compensation that had been rejected included women who had suffered from tuberculosis, debility, anaemia or neurasthenia.[57] It was agreed that claims would only be admitted for TB if, in medical opinion, the woman's conditions of service aggravated the illness. For the other illnesses cited, claims would only be admitted if the woman had been subjected to greater strain than fellow colleagues.

The WAAC subsequently put forward a number of test cases to the War Office but was unsuccessful as witnesses were required and these had been demobilised and were difficult to find. The Corps was also aggrieved that as many of the women were not 'ordinarily employed persons' they were not considered as deserving of compensation. Their argument was that the women had suffered illness or injury while employed, and that after the war many were reliant on their income.[58] The Corps were concerned that a process would not be ready in time for the disbandment of the Corps on 30 April 1920 and indeed no changes were made.

In July 1920, the Office of the Parish Council in Dunfermline wrote to their MP, John Wallace. They had passed a resolution that strongly protested against the unreasonable and continued refusal of the government to recognise the claims of ex-service women to the benefits available under the Pensions Royal Warrant. They stated that such patriotic women were enduring needless suffering and relied on charitable sources or outdoor relief from Parish Councils. The Ministry of Pensions replied that they would not revisit the matter. As late as 1939, an ex-WAAC who had emigrated to Canada wrote to Queen Elizabeth (consort to George VI) enquiring about compensation after being discharged as medically unfit in 1918. She stated that she had been too ill in 1918 to deal with the matter but, at the time of writing, she was often hungry and cold and wanted to return to England. She did not believe that she would require a pension for many more years as she considered that she did not have long to live.[59] The matter was referred to the War Office but the files do not contain any record of the final decision that was made. It is likely that her application would have been refused, as cases needed to be referred as soon after discharge as possible.

Mentions in Dispatches, Awards and Medals

On 24 December 1917, the WAAC was first recorded in Haig's List of Mentions – a list of names deserving special mention. The ten names included those of an area controller, administrators and workers.

Members of the Corps received awards both during and after the war. In January 1918, Florence Leach and Gwynne-Vaughan were appointed Commanders of the Most Excellent Order of the British Empire (CBE). Gwynne-Vaughan's CBE was listed in the Military Section and she was therefore the first woman to wear the insignia of a Military Commander of the Order of the British Empire. In 1919, both women were appointed Dames Commander of the Order of the British Empire (DBE).

On 31 May 1920, forty members of the WAAC received the OBE at an Investiture at Wellington Barracks, London. Many more received honours at Investitures in other parts of the country.

In September 1921, it was announced that all British War and Victory medals awarded to WAACs who had served overseas were available for distribution.

Women's Future in the Military

The WAAC had ceased to exist and it was clear that in a way similar to other women's war work, the change in their circumstances had been exceptional for the period of the war. Women were no longer urgently wanted as the war propaganda had proclaimed. Some women were content and willing to return to their homes or former employment but others wanted to continue working with the Army.

There is an argument that the WAAC and women in the Air Force and Navy paved the way for future female military service. The counter argument is that gender divisions were reinforced as the women took on mainly feminine roles and were not involved in combat, although they were exposed to air raids and privation. Indeed, some of the occupations available to women outside of the WAAC, for example in heavy industry, the railways or agriculture, could have been seen as more strenuous.

In 1918, the writer Ethel Tweedie in her book *Women and Soldiers* wrote that women were willing to fight rather than remain in an auxiliary capacity:

> The men of Britain, being men, want women's help in all things but one – the shambles. "You shall toil for us, scheme for us, nurse us, succour us in a thousand ways; but you shall not redden a Boche bayonet with your blood. … " Well, we women don't agree with you – won't agree with you … if our country wants us we shall go and fight. The writer is ready to form A WOMEN'S BATTALION, the moment it becomes necessary for women to fill that fighting breach. … One penned the phrase *A Woman's Army* almost nervously in 1914, little dreaming that in a year it would be on every one's lips. One writes *A Women's Fighting Battalion* almost shyly in 1918: well, a year may see many such battalions ready for the trenches.[60]

There is no evidence in primary sources that women in the WAAC were willing to fight and the War Office had absolutely no intention of considering the matter.

The WAAC was not seamlessly superseded by another corps of women working alongside, or within, the Army. In August 1919, the Army Council had considered retaining 10,000 women in the Army and Air Force but this was rejected. In 1920, a Women's Reserve Sub-Committee was established. It was chaired by General Burnett-Hitchcock, and membership included Gwynne-Vaughan and Florence Leach. They recommended that a Women's Reserve be established as part of the Territorial Army. This was not progressed by the Army Council, partly due to a lack of funds.

In June 1921, the Army Council once again decided against forming a Women's Reserve. They acknowledged their potential role in national emergencies but did not mention the possibility of future war.

The OCA Gazette reported that this was met by ex-service women with disappointment and it was 'not the official recognition which the Service Women's organisations deserved.'[61] In the meantime, the Women's Legion Transport Section and the FANY continued as voluntary organisations.

In 1936, Gwynne-Vaughan was one of the ex-service women on the committee of the Emergency Service, set up to train women as officers if the need for a women's unit in a national emergency were to arise. The Emergency Service was superseded by the formation of the Auxiliary Territorial Service (ATS) on 9 September 1938 but it was not officially closed down until March 1939. Gwynne-Vaughan, representing the Emergency Service, was a member of the Advisory Council that designed the new scheme. The discussions were very similar to those held in 1917 prior to the formation of the WAAC. Many of the proposals put forward by Gwynne-Vaughan and her female counterparts, based on their considerable experience, were initially disregarded, for example enlistment rather than enrolment, medical examinations and commissioned officers. This demonstrates that the WAAC was not viewed by the Army Council as the foundation of a subsequent Women's Corps. Indeed, it is as if the WAAC had not existed and old prejudices remained.

On 3 July 1939 Gwynne-Vaughan was appointed Director ATS, with the rank of chief controller. In the first year, she dealt with many of the same issues as she had with the WAAC: status; discipline; pay; rank badges; medical care; accommodation (including in France); and the mixing of men and women. It was not until April 1941 that the ATS was awarded full military status. As a result, pay was revised, women officers were commissioned and were permitted to wear officers' badges of crown and star. There remained, however, differences between the men and women in the application of military law in terms of punishment, for example the major penalties were not employed. Gwynne-Vaughan held a commission for only a month as she retired shortly after the announcement. Gwynne-Vaughan had worked tirelessly to establish a place for women in the Army. However, this was within the context of an auxiliary role. In her autobiography published in 1942, Gwynne-Vaughan asserted that women lacked physical strength, fighting was the job of men, the appropriate place for women in the Army was carrying out background duties and 'babies apart, there is probably no more primitively feminine job than to cook for the fighting man.'[62] She set out the three conditions for the successful employment of women in the Auxiliary Services as follows: trained women officers and NCOs should be in charge of them; their conditions of service should be as similar as possible to that of the men; and due regard paid to the needs of the family.[63] In consideration of the future, Gwynne-Vaughan believed that women serving with the Army should be enlisted as members of the corps they served rather than as a separate service.

In February 1949, the Women's Royal Army Corps (WRAC) received Royal Assent and the women were subject to the Army Act in its entirety. Although initially organised as independent companies, they eventually followed the model envisioned by Gwynne-Vaughan and became integrated with the units with which they worked. Members of the Corps served in Northern Ireland, the Falklands, the Gulf (1990–91) and Iraq (1991). The WRAC was disbanded in 1992 and held its Disbandment service in Guildford Cathedral in the presence of Queen Elizabeth The Queen Mother (Commandant in Chief) and the Duchess of Kent (Controller Commandant).

Women in the British Army serve on the front line, but until recently, they were banned from serving in front line infantry roles. This was in contrast to women in the armed services in a number of countries, for example the United States of America, Canada, Australia and France. In December 2014, a review by the British Armed Forces of women in Ground Close Combat (GCC) roles, recommended that the government adopt a positive approach to the matter and conduct further physiological research. In July 2016, the prime minister announced the lifting of the ban.

Suffrage and the Vote

As well as the relationship between the Corps and the future of women in the military, it is important to consider the WAAC in the wider context of citizenship. Prior to the First World War, a link was made between women's suffrage, citizenship and national defence. It was considered by anti-suffrage campaigners that women should not be eligible to vote because they did not engage in the defence of their country and were therefore not full citizens. At the outbreak of war, some suffrage societies, for example, the Women's Social and Political Union (WSPU) suspended their activities and concentrated on supporting the government and the war effort. Christabel Pankhurst of the WSPU believed that once the war was over it would be difficult for the government to refuse to acknowledge the role that women had undertaken and, consequently, their right to the vote. In subsequent decades there has been debate as to the extent to which women's involvement in war work facilitated the passing of the Representation of the People Act 1918. The consensus is that it had little impact and that the Act would have been passed in any case due to the progress made by women's suffrage organisations in the decades before the war. Indeed, as suffrage was only granted to women over 30 years of age, many of the young women who had worked on the Home Front or overseas would not have been eligible to vote. In 1918, approximately 8,500,000 women were registered to vote. Of these, 3,372 women who were serving in the armed services were registered as navy and military voters and this number would have included military nurses, as well as WAAC and WRNS. Although men could not vote unless they were 21 years of age, if they had turned 19 when in service as part of the war they were also able to vote. In line with women at home, those women serving in the British military overseas could only vote if they were over 30 years of age.

Chapter 8

Memory

Imperial War Museum – Women's Work Sub-Committee

On 5 March 1917, the proposal by Sir Alfred Mond MP (Swansea) for a National War Museum was approved by the War Cabinet. It was renamed the Imperial War Museum (IWM) later that year. The museum was headed by a committee, which, with the support of sub-committees, was responsible for developing the collections. One of the sub-committees was the Women's Work Sub-Committee (WWSC), chaired by Lady Priscilla Norman and with Agnes Conway as the Honorary Secretary. Lady Priscilla Norman had run a hospital in France during the first few months of the war. Other members included Lady Mond, Lady Haig, and Lady Askwith.

The WWSC oversaw the Women's Work Section (WWS), also referred to as the Women's Section. From 1917, it collected material relating to women's contribution to the war. For the WAAC this included letters, diaries, books, ephemera, photographs, medals, artwork, uniform and film. This formed part of the wider Women's Work Collection.

The museum did not have its own premises until 1920. The first formal exhibition was held at Burlington House in London for two months from 7 January 1918. The entrance fee was 1/- and all proceeds went to the Joint War Committee of the BRCS and the Order of St John. It included an exhibit of women's war work and was visited by Queen Alexandra and Princess Victoria, as well as Sergeant Major Flora Sandes who had fought with the Serbian Army. The women's war work exhibit included a recruitment drive for the WAAC.

On 13 February 1918, Lady Priscilla Norman wrote to Chalmers Watson after her resignation, requesting records for inclusion in the Women's Section stating that '[i]t is most important that documents relating to the WAAC should be preserved for posterity and the beginnings of a movement are always of special interest.'[1] A couple of months later, Lady Priscilla Norman wrote to Florence Leach that the museum still did not have archive material for the WAAC and was most anxious that the Corps be represented.[2] In July 1918 a selection of papers were made available for the WWSC to view at the Corps headquarters in Grosvenor Street and copies were subsequently lodged with the museum archive.

On 26 August 1918, Agnes Conway wrote to Florence Leach requesting that she forward letters to the next of kin of the nine women who had died in the bombing raid on the night of 29 – 30 May 1918.[3] The letters requested that they provide a cabinet photograph of each woman. It is moving to read the responses, in which the families were both keen to be of assistance and concerned that they met the WWSC requirements. Jeanie Watson's mother – Jeanie Oliphant – wrote 'I enclose the photograph of my daughter Miss Jeanie Watson. Sorry that it is the only one I have got of her. I hope that it will suit all right. If not would you please return some time.'[4] Lady Priscilla Norman also wrote to Florence Leach for a photograph of her sister, Violet Long, who had drowned that same month on her return to England.[5]

On 9 October 1918, the WWSC held its own exhibition. The Women's War Services Exhibition opened to the public at the Whitechapel Gallery in London and charged no admission fee. Lady Priscilla Norman invited Chalmers Watson and Florence Leach to a private viewing of the exhibition prior to opening. The ground floor included plaster models, uniformed mannequins and photographs showing the wide variety of work carried out by women, from munitions and nursing to lamplighters and tram conductresses, as well as the WAAC. It also housed the Women's War Shrine, which was dedicated to the 500 women who had died on war service by that time, including the WAAC at Abbeville. The cabinet photographs, requested from next of kin by the WWSC, were displayed on the shrine. The shrine, behind permanently opened black drapes, consisted of an alter adorned with candles, flowers, flags and medals. The upstairs gallery was organised by the Ministry of Labour and housed, amongst other exhibits, a life-size model of a cow to assist in demonstrating the work of the Women's Land Army. In total, 82,000 people, including Queen Mary and Princess Mary, visited the exhibition during the following six weeks. The WWSC asked Florence Leach whether the Corps would donate the WAAC material in the exhibition to the museum. Permission was sought from the War Office and the material, including uniforms, was donated to the museum.

The WWSC continued to collect material during 1919, writing to all WAAC controllers and asking for personal accounts written either by them or their administrators, as well as a photographic portrait. They did not ask for accounts or photographs from other grades. The Corps headquarters in London closed on 30 April 1920 and many of its records and documents were lodged with the WWS.

The IWM opened at the Crystal Palace in June 1920. Lady Priscilla Norman invited Florence Leach to the grand opening on 7 July 1920 'in order that representative women may be present at the ceremony.'[6]

In 1920, the WWSC received the nominal roll of deceased officials and members of the WAAC. They subsequently collected photographs of the deceased, as well as WAACs who had received decorations.

Further material on the WAAC has subsequently been collected by the IWM, including a number of interviews recorded in the 1970s.

WAAC in Photographs

The photographs for the exhibition at the Whitechapel Gallery, which were mainly of women's war work in the UK, including the WAAC, were taken by two male photographers – Horace Nicholls and George Parham Lewis.

In October 1918, the WWSC commissioned the photographer Olive Edis to record women's service overseas, including the WAACs in their camps and places of work. Olive Edis was 43 years old and an established portrait artist. She was to be the only female official war photographer of the First World War and was the fifth photographer to be appointed. Her permit was initially refused by Lieutenant Colonel A.N. Lee, who organised and censored war artists and photographers in France. He later explained to her that this was due both to the Armistice and a lack of transport for her use.[7] The permit was eventually granted and Olive Edis arrived in France on 2 March 1919, accompanied by Lady Priscilla Norman and Agnes Conway. Their presence would have greatly assisted Olive Edis in obtaining access to the WAAC due to their strong relationship with the Chief Controller.

Work commenced on 3 March 1919 and the month-long tour included Calais, Boulogne, Le Havre, Abbeville, Étaples, Dieppe, Harfleur and Bourges. Olive Edis took photographs in a variety of work places, from the OBOS to the Signals, as well as the printers and cemeteries. She expressed regret at not being able to photograph the WAAC at the bakery in Dieppe because the women worked nights and had left for the day by the time that she arrived.[8] Olive Edis also took photographs in the WAAC camps, including the women playing football and a chapel within a YWCA hut.

Part way through the tour she met with Lieutenant Colonel A.N. Lee and wrote in her diary of their encounter:

> He was a little inclined to challenge the need of my coming, and showed us volumes of 5 by 4 photos, many taken in the women's camps, by the official photographers. However, I explained that the Imperial War Museum thought that a woman photographer, living among the girls in their camps, was likely to achieve more intimate pictures, more descriptive of their everyday life, than a man press photographer. He quite saw the point ...[9]

There are approximately forty-five photographs of the WAAC by Olive Edis held by the IWM. The images are documentary in style rather than the propaganda of those taken of the women by male photographers during the war. In many cases, the women are not looking at the camera and although the women are posed, the result is an impression that the photographer is observing them while they work. Olive Edis wrote of the welcome she received by the WAAC officials and photographed a number of them.

In April 1919, the WWSC sent copies of the photographs to Florence Leach for approval and in May 1919 they were sent to the featured units so that the women could purchase copies for a small fee.

WAAC in Art

The WAAC in France was the subject of a number of art works commissioned by the IWM from male and female artists: Sir William Orpen; Beatrice Lithiby; Sir John Lavery; Austin Spare; and Geneste Beeton.

On 10 August 1918, Gwynne-Vaughan had an interview at WAAC headquarters in St Valery-sur-Somme with Sir William Orpen regarding a portrait which had been commissioned by the IWM.[10] This was shortly before she left the Corps. There followed a number of sittings and Gwynne-Vaughan considered him to be an interesting guest and enjoyed his stories of what he had seen on his painting tour of the Western Front. Gwynne-Vaughan later wrote that 'of its excellence I will only say that an orderly, entering the room in which it stood, came smartly to attention under the impression that the original was sitting there.'[11] The oil painting is held by the IWM.[12]

In January 1919, in a letter informing Florence Leach that Olive Edis would be an official photographer, the WWSC also stated their intention to send out an official war artist. They wanted to record the women disembarking from transport, tending graves and working with the US Army.[13] By coincidence, that same month, Florence Leach received a letter from Beatrice Lithiby who not only was a serving member of the WAAC in the UK but also an artist who had studied at the London Academy Schools. Beatrice Lithiby was keen to perpetuate the memory of the Corps through a pictorial record. In

February 1919, the Committee met with Beatrice Lithiby and wrote to Florence Leach that 'this would be an excellent way of procuring an artist who thoroughly understands the work of the QMAAC.'[14] After reviewing a sample of Beatrice Lithiby's work, particularly a watercolour of WAACs working in a kitchen, they agreed that she should be employed to record the work of the WAAC in France. There was an initial disagreement between the War Office and IWM as to which should fund her time in France but this was resolved by Florence Leach and aided by Beatrice Lithiby's agreement to be paid £120 a year by the War Office rather than £175.[15] The IWM did provide funding for her materials.

Beatrice Lithiby travelled to France in May 1919. While she was there, her father travelled back and forth to visit her. He took her finished paintings to Lady Priscilla Norman but carried them with him on his return visits to France because, by showing them to the officials at subsequent locations, she was able to generate greater interest in her work and secure better facilities. The sixteen watercolours finally obtained by the WWSC, included WAACs engaged in work, for example as telephonists and mechanics. There were also a number that showed the interior of the Nissen huts in which the women lived, as well as a YWCA hut. As described in Chapter 3, the personalisation of their quarters was important to the women and this would have been appreciated by Beatrice Lithiby.

After demobilisation, she continued to play an active role amongst ex-WAACs. In 1923, she was asked to produce a membership card on vellum to be presented to Queen Mary on the occasion of her joining the ex-Service Women's Club. She led sixty members of the OCA in the 1934 Armistice Parade in London. In addition to serving in the First World War, for which she was awarded the MBE, Beatrice Lithiby served as an officer in the ATS during the Second World War, for which she was awarded the OBE.

In February 1919, the WWSC commissioned a further artist, Sir John Lavery, to record the Women's Services in France. He had been working as an official war artist in the UK for many months and was resting in Tunisia. He agreed to take up his commission on his return in May 1919. In the interim, the WWSC gave some thought to potential subjects. During April 1919, Lady Priscilla Norman wrote to Florence Leach agreeing with her suggestion that a Review of the Corps would make an excellent subject for a painting and that she consider featuring in the picture along with senior colleagues, including Chief Controller Lila Davy. Lady Priscilla Norman also wrote to Laura Knight asking her to consider painting the bakeries at Dieppe which Olive Edis had not photographed.[16] The latter came to nothing and the request was passed to Sir John Lavery. Laura Knight later became a Dame and was commissioned by the IWM as an official war artist in the Second World War.

Sir John Lavery spent two months touring camps and places of work, including those of the WAAC in Étaples, Dieppe and Boulogne. His works ranged from WAACs at work in the cemetery at Étaples to the convalescent home in Le Touquet and the bakeries in Dieppe. During this time, the WWSC wrote a number of letters to Lila Davy, as well as to her deputies in Calais and Le Havre, trying to track Sir John Lavery down and repeating their request for a painting of a Review. In June 1919, he was eventually located in Boulogne and Lila Davy reported to the WWSC that not only was a review impossible to organise but that Sir John Lavery did not believe it to be a suitable subject.[17] The WWSC was disappointed but in February 1920 they viewed the paintings that he had produced and bought a number at a reduced cost. Lila Davy wrote in her War Diary on 21 May 1919 that she sat for her portrait and that Sir John Lavery left the following day.[18] However, there is no record of the portrait in the IWM catalogue and its whereabouts are unknown. It is possible that the portrait was either not completed or it remains in private ownership.

In April 1919, the WWSC wrote to the WAAC deputy controller in Boulogne that they were sending an artist, Austin Spare, to the area and hoped that he would record the WAAC working in Terlincthun Cemetery. Staff Sergeant Spare was an official war artist for the RAMC. The IWM holds a painting by Austin Spare titled *Queen Mary's Army*

Auxiliary Corps: Tending Graves at Wimereux Cemetery.[19] Terlincthun is located north of Boulogne.

The WWSC commissioned the artist Geneste Beeton in 1920. They purchased one painting titled *Miss Penrose, MM, QMAAC Administrator; Superintending French labour on camouflage at Aire.*[20] This is, in fact, a portrait of the artist. Geneste Beeton's maiden name was Penrose. She was one of three female artists who were assistant administrators in the Corps and ran camouflage units in France. Geneste Beeton was awarded the MM in April 1919 for her behaviour under shell fire during the Spring Offensive which resulted in most of the 400 French women remaining at their posts at the Royal Engineers Northern Special Works Park.[21]

WAAC in Written Works

There is little representation of women's war work in novels written between 1914 and 1939, or within subsequent historical novels. A key factor is that the majority were written by middle class authors from a middle class point of view. There are two novels which feature WAACs as main characters. The first is Bessie Marchant's *A Transport Girl in France: A Story of the Adventures of a WAAC*, which was published in 1919.[22] It is a romantic adventure written for girls and not an accurate representation of life as a WAAC. It was not until 1930 that the WAAC featured in a literary novel – *Not So Quiet: Stepdaughters of War* by Evadne Price, who wrote under the pseudonym Helen Zenna Smith.[23] It portrays the experience of middle and upper class female ambulance drivers in France and is based on contemporary diaries. The protagonist, Smithy, latterly joins the WAAC. The late 1920s and early 1930s saw a boom in the publishing of First World War novels. These were often semi-autobiographical and although not always overtly pacifist in nature, their realistic descriptions of the horrors of war meant that they could not be accused of promoting or glorifying it. *Not So Quiet: Stepdaughters of War* is an anti-war novel which uses female workers to underline the differences between propaganda fed to the civilians on the Home Front and the reality of war on the front line.

Smithy purposely enrols as a worker in the WAAC with the intention of upsetting her mother and imagines her response:

> My daughter a common W.A.A.C., a domestic worker, mixing with dreadful people out of the slums, some of them really *are*, you know. And I've even heard some of them are immoral – babies and all that kind of thing. My daughter not even an *officer*, and she could have enlisted with the very best people.[24]

The rumours about the WAAC, albeit proved false, had not been forgotten. The character Smithy observes her new WAAC friends from the lower classes through her middle class eyes but is very fond of them. The novel ends with a fatal air raid in which Smithy survives and serves as a reminder to the reader of the sacrifices made by women during the war. The novelist herself worked in munitions and at the Air Ministry. Unlike many of her male counterparts, Evadne Price would not see her work re-printed within her lifetime. *Not So Quiet: Stepdaughters of War* was re-printed in 1989 by the Feminist Press.[25]

There are three other books about the WAAC, published between 1918 and 1930, which are not fiction but autobiography or contemporary account. A collection of letters sent home by a WAAC were published anonymously in 1918 under the title *The Letters of Thomasina Atkins*.[26] The author was a clerk and makes a number of references to class. In a letter written before leaving England, she writes '[t]here are hundreds of girls here, mostly of the factory and the domestic-servant class. Such priceless accents! And oh! such odd faces – just like a Phil May panorama.'[27] Phil May was a caricaturist. Later she writes of how she mixed with women from other classes during meal times:

> I try to fall in for meals with the nicest of the girls, but it can't always be managed. Yesterday I had to hurry, and found myself with a munitioner on my right, a charwoman on my left, and two

tough little mechanics in front – but I didn't even have indigestion. Perhaps I am a red tie Socialist after all. One thing, whatever the grade or habit of life, all these women are really gold at heart. Some nine carat, I grant you; some twenty two; but the precious core is there alright – it is simply up to one to tunnel through.[28]

The second book, *"Johnnie" of QMAAC*[29], is the biography of Elizabeth Johnston, a signaller based in Rouen who was from Anstruther, Scotland. She had originally wanted to be a motor driver in France and acquired the necessary qualifications, as well as learning French at evening class. Due to her parents' concern regarding the potential dangers inherent in such a job, she opted to be a telephonist in the WAAC. Before she left for France, she wrote '[o]f course, I have counted the cost, and if death should come to me out there, why then, THEN I SHALL KNOW THE GREAT SECRET.'[30] Elizabeth died on Christmas Day 1918 aged 27, after falling from the tower of St Ouen Church, Rouen. She had come off a night shift and rather than go to the Cathedral service, she evidently changed her plans and visited the church. The reason for her fall was never determined, but it was believed that she had a dizzy spell while sitting on a low balustrade encircling the gallery. Her unconscious body was found by an English soldier and two American soldiers on the roof of a chapel beneath the tower. Aid was administered at the scene but she passed away on arrival at No 8 Stationary Hospital where she had previously been admitted with influenza. Elizabeth was buried at St Severs Cemetery in Rouen with military honours. She had once mentioned that she would like the St Andrew's flag laid on her coffin and this wish was fulfilled. A few months before her death, she had written home of her visit to the cemetery with a friend, telling them how it was maintained so beautifully by WAAC gardeners. Agnes Anderson, a friend of Elizabeth, compiled the book using Elizabeth's diary, poems and letters home.

The third book is *Eve in Khaki* by Edith Barton and Marguerite Cody, which was published in the spring of 1918.[31] Edith Barton wrote of the WAAC in the UK while Maguerite Cody travelled to France.

The account was positive and intended to encourage recruitment. At the end of the book Marguerite Cody wrote that:

> The feeling of admiration with which I left the W.A.A.C. in France was, I must confess it now, faintly tinged with disappointment – disappointment not in those who have gone over, but in the women at home who have stayed behind. Perhaps they are not slackers. They may be doing work in hospitals or in offices, but is it not work that others could do as well who have ties which keep them at home?[32]

In 1930 a fourth book, written by an anonymous author, titled *WAAC: The Woman's Story of the War* was published.[33] Despite the title, the protagonist was a VAD and ambulance driver and there is little written of the WAAC. The OCA Gazette was not impressed by the publication and wrote '[y]ou will wonder what this all has to do with Q.M.A.A.C. Very little. This V.A.D. just chose "W.A.A.C." in order to have a very attractive title to her book.'[34]

In 1920, Richard Aldington, who had served in the First World War, published an anti-war novel titled *Death of a Hero*.[35] The novel is antagonistic towards women. In 1930, the OCA Gazette reported that a number of members had complained about Richard Aldington's references in his novel to the WAAC based in Étaples. Gwynne-Vaughan considered the matter serious enough to engage a solicitor and Richard Aldington agreed that the offending passage be removed from future editions.[36]

The author Winifred Holtby, who had experienced the German attack on Whitby in 1914, served from September 1918 as hostel forewoman for a Signals unit in Huchenneville. She shared a cottage with an administrator, Jean McWilliam, who became a close friend. Winifred's post-war letters to Jean were published, after Winifred's death at the young age of 35, as *Letters to a Friend*.[37] Although she attempted to write a book while in France based on her experiences, titled *The Forest Unit*[38], it was never published. Charlotte Bottomley's fiancé worked at Huchenneville and she understood from him that Winifred Holtby was very popular there because of the ghost stories that she read aloud.[39] Vera Brittain wrote of her friend's experiences in *Testament of Friendship: The Story of Winifred Holtby*.[40]

On 14 April 1917, Gwynne-Vaughan interviewed the novelist Cicely Hamilton and recommended her as a unit administrator but she did not take up a post.[41] Cicely Hamilton did submit articles to newspapers, including *The Morning Post*, which described WAAC life in France.

In September 1918, Erskine Macdonald Ltd published *Ripples from the Ranks of the Q.M.A.A.C.* by 3617, I. Grindlay.[42] The book contains forty poems written by a member of the WAAC which cover her experiences on service in Edinburgh, Scotland. The topics range from the patriotic call to serve in the Corps to the discomfort of route marches and army pay. There is no trace of the poet in the WAAC records either by her name or army number and it is probable that her records are among those lost in the Second World War. It is highly likely that I. Grindlay was from Canada, as one of her poems titled *Day-Dream*, refers to her returning home to Alberta at the end of the war. Further research suggests that I. Grindlay may be Isa Grindlay, a Canadian poet. Isa Grindlay was born Isabella Stevenson in 1884 in Stirlingshire, Scotland. She emigrated to Alberta, Canada in 1910 where she married Charles Grindlay, who subsequently died in France in 1916. This book of poetry has not previously been attributed to Isa Grindlay.

Old Comrades Associations

The QMAAC OCA, affiliated to the Service Women's Association, was established in December 1919 and registered as a limited company on 25 March 1922. Queen Mary gave permission for the continued association of her name with the OCA when it was registered as a limited company. The OCA headquarters were housed in the Duke of York's headquarters, Kensington and Chelsea, London. The first elected Board of Directors included the President Florence Simpson (formerly Leach), Lila Davy and a number of former officials. Gwynne-Vaughan did not join the Board until 1929, although she was one of the Vice Presidents on its Committee from 1919. In December 1920, there were 3,000 members and forty local branches.[43] There was a steady increase in membership during 1921.

The main objectives of the OCA were to:

> Assist both financially and otherwise all women and girls of good character who were members of the Queen Mary's Army Auxiliary Corps or any other Corps formed … for service of women; to enable them to procure a livelihood and settle down as self-dependent citizens of the British Empire and to promote their spiritual, educational and physical welfare. To maintain the strong and united comradeship which exists between all those who have served in the … Corps and to benefit the Members as far as is possible and reasonable.[44]

To that end, a QMAAC Benevolent Fund was set up and administered by a sub-committee of the OCA. This was important in light of the fact that the WAACs did not receive a pension and in many cases, had considerable difficulty in obtaining compensation for illness or injury directly attributable to their war service. In 1920, the OCA reported that the fund was depleted and there was no means of increasing it.[45] By December 1920, 150 cases had been administered.[46] However, as membership increased in 1921 so did the funds. By 1924, membership dropped away and by 1925 had fallen to 1,300.[47] In 1926, following a concerted effort to recruit more members, numbers rose to 2,181.[48] The subsequent increase in funds enabled 223 women to receive financial assistance from the QMAAC Benevolent Fund that year. In 1929, the OCA was able to assist in 324 cases.[49] Examples of the way in which the funds were spent included training, assistance to emigrate and the purchase of food during sickness or a period of convalescence. In one case, where an ex-WAAC had re-trained to become a midwife, the OCA paid for her uniform. Ex-service women were also entitled to apply for financial assistance from the Service Women's Benevolent Fund.

The OCA was open to all grades and the members were liable for a yearly subscription. A periodical entitled *The Gazette* was published monthly from July 1920. These publications provide a fascinating insight into the lives of many ex-WAACs after the war and the way in which they continued to feel part of the Corps. The first reunion dinner for officials was held on 25 July 1920. There was also an annual dinner held in London, often at Derry and Toms, for all grades, which was attended by hundreds of ex-WAACs. Nora Barker initially went every year, stopping once she married and had children but returning in latter years.[50] The QMAAC Old Comrades' Club and hostel in Belgrave Road, London, at which dancing, games and a canteen were available, was open daily and reunions held every Thursday evening. Local branches were set up at home and overseas and ran social and sports events that raised funds for the OCA. A summer camp was held in 1920 on Ham Island, on the River Thames in Old Windsor, Berkshire, England. The following year this was turned into a permanent holiday and rest camp. The camp was named *Shanghai-on-Thames* as it was made possible due to donations from the Shanghai Race Club of which an ex-WAAC was a member. The women stayed in a wooden hut, reminiscent of those in which they had lived in France.

The OCA had originally decided to become a limited company in order to protect the Committee against financial liability. In 1931, the Board officially commenced the voluntary winding up of the Association as a company. They considered that due to the increased complexities of company law, being a limited company was both expensive and inconvenient.[51]

In 1940, membership of the OCA was extended to ex-members of the ATS. In 1941, when it was extended to serving members, the Princess Royal (Controller Commandant ATS) and Jean Knox (Chief Controller ATS) became respectively Honorary President and a Vice-President of the OCA. In 1942, the QMAAC OCA was superseded by the QMAAC and ATS Comrades Association. In 1949, this was in turn superseded by the WRAC Association. The objectives of the latter are: to maintain contact between former members; foster mutual friendship between them and provide for social gatherings; foster esprit de corps, comradeship and welfare; and preserve traditions, including those of the WAAC and QMAAC.

In March 1967, the WRAC Association held a reunion dinner to commemorate fifty years since the WAAC had embarked for France. Gwynne-Vaughan, aged 88, addressed the 100 or so members in attendance. She passed away in her sleep five months later on 26 August 1967 at Sussexdown, an RAF Convalescent Home.

In the same year, Colonel Julia Cowper's *A Short History of Queen Mary's Army Auxiliary Corps*[52] was published by the WRAC Association to mark the fiftieth anniversary of the formation of the WAAC in 1917 and as a tribute to their work during the First World War.

Memorials and Remembrance

At the beginning of 1923, at a meeting of women in York, it was decided to raise money to restore the Five Sisters Window in York Minster in memory of the women who had died in service with the Allied Armed Forces during the war.[53] The idea had originally been put forward by a woman named Helen Little, who lived in the city. The OCA contributed towards the £3,000 fund. In addition, the names of the 1,465 women were inscribed on the oak panels of the Women's National Memorial Screen surrounding the Chapel of St Nicholas. On 24 June 1925, the restored window was unveiled by the Duchess of York and the screen was dedicated by the Archbishop of York. OCA members, led by Florence Simpson, attended the service. The OCA Gazette reported Florence Simpson as having stated that:

Now at last achievement had been found of a wish that had long been felt – that they should have a Roll of Honour in some sacred building in this country. They had tried in many places to get a tablet erected, but up to now they had had no Roll of Honour except in their hearts, but now, as the Archbishop of York had said, the old Mother had taken her daughters to her heart and would infold [sic] them with her silence and her peace.[54]

A couple of years previously, the OCA had set aside a fund for a permanent memorial and considered placing it in the Duke of York's Chapel in Chelsea, London but the plan was not realised.

In 1926, OCA members attended the dedication of a chapel in Holy Trinity Church, Grays Inn Road, London, to the memory of 'The Brave Women of the War.'[55] Holy Trinity Church was closed in 1928.

The names of the nine women who were killed at Abbeville are recorded on their local war memorials. The Scottish women (M. Blaikley, B. Campbell, C. Connor, J. Grant and J. Watson) are included in the Roll of Honour at the Scottish National War Memorial at Edinburgh Castle, Scotland. The memorial was officially opened in July 1927 by the Prince of Wales and the service attended by Chalmers Watson.

Violet Long, who drowned in the Channel and whose body was never found, is remembered at the Hollybrook Memorial in Southampton which is dedicated to the missing, including those who lost their lives at sea in hospital ships and transport.

The ATS and the WRAC have had strong connections with Guildford since the 1940s. During the construction of the Cathedral, WRAC recruits were taken to the site on Stag Hill to 'buy a brick.' This scheme was introduced to fund the build. At a cost of 2/6, members of the public were able to purchase a brick made of clay dug from Stag Hill and have their name inscribed on it. In October 1955, the Secretary of the Guildford New Cathedral Fund (Miss Eleanor Iredale) wrote to the Director of the WRAC (Brigadier Mary Railton). She asked whether the WRAC might wish to fund the installation of a window in the Nave as a memorial to officers and members of the Corps.[56] The estimated cost of the window was £1,000. The Brigadier accepted the proposal in principle and wrote to the four commands to enquire as to the amount of money they anticipated that they would be able to raise. The following January, the commands responded in agreement to the proposal, except for HQ Scotland as half of the unit commanders believed that as few members would worship or visit the Cathedral when it opened, any funds would be better spent on the Chapel at the WRAC camp in Guildford. The Brigadier emphasised the close association with the city and the Corps committed to raising the funds by the end of January 1957. The window was designed by Moira Forsyth, a renowned stained glass artist, in consultation with the Corps. It consisted of the WRAC badge, as well as the Corps motto, 'Gentle in Manner, Resolute in Deed'. The WRAC raised £2,537 2/6, which allowed them to also fund two small windows under the main window and the statue of *Faith* by John Cobbett, built into the exterior of the window. A cheque for the funds was handed to the Cathedral at a short ceremony on 1 June 1957, followed by a concert by the WRAC Band. The glass was displayed at the ceremony, albeit the window in the Nave was not ready to receive it. The attendees were able to enter the Nave under construction and were the first members of the public allowed to do so.[57] The glass was installed in 1961 and unveiled at a ceremony in September of that year. On 16 April 1994, a commemorative window, which incorporated the badges of the WAAC, QMAAC, ATS and WRAC, was unveiled in the Cathedral by the Duchess of Kent. A memorial stone laid in the floor beneath the window was unveiled on the same day. It reads 'To commemorate those who served in these Women's Corps and their association with Guildford.' Photographs of the WAAC and QMAAC badges within the window, as well as the statue of *Faith*, can be found at plate eight.

Guildford Cathedral also houses the WAAC and QMAAC Books of Remembrance, as well as those for the ATS and WRAC. The Book for the WAAC and QMAAC is a copy of the Commonwealth War Graves Commission (CWGC) record. On 26 March 2014, the WRAC Association installed a Memorial Cabinet in which the Books are displayed. The Memorial Cabinet was blessed at a service on 15 April 2014, conducted by the Dean of Guildford.

There is one national memorial to the women who served in the WAAC. This is located at the National Memorial Arboretum in Staffordshire and is dedicated to the women who served in the WAAC, QMAAC, ATS and WRAC in both world wars.

The WAAC took part in the Peace Parade in 1919 and the flag that they carried was later kept at the headquarters of the OCA. In 1920, members of the OCA took part in the Armistice Parade in London, as well as visiting the Tomb of the Unknown Soldier. The women wore their uniform for the occasion. The women attended every year and laid a wreath but in 1927 the arrangements changed and ex-service women were officially represented in the Parade. Sixty members of the OCA attended and it was requested that they did not wear their uniform, rather civilian clothes.

The sixtieth anniversary of the formation of the WAAC was marked at the Combined Women's Services Diamond Jubilee Service at Westminster Abbey on 3 March 1977. Serving members of the WRAC, WRAF and WRNS marched with veterans of both world wars. The service was attended by Queen Elizabeth The Queen Mother, Princess Anne, the Duchess of Kent and Princess Alice. Many of the WAAC who attended signed a copy of the Westminster Abbey Nine Hundred Years Commemorative Book, which has since been lodged with the IWM. Nora Barker attended and referred to it as a great occasion.[58]

On 20 May 2012, the WRAC Association attended a Service of Rededication at Guildford Cathedral, at which the QMAAC and ATS Standards were laid up. They are kept in the Gallery alongside other Regimental Standards.

The WRAC Association attends the annual Cenotaph Service and Parade organised by the Royal British Legion on Remembrance Sunday. The WRAC Association hopes that in 2017, to commemorate the 100th anniversary of the formation of the WAAC, the Royal British Legion will permit the WRAC Association National Standard to be paraded at the Festival of Remembrance at the Royal Albert Hall. On the 18 March 2017, the WRAC Association plans to hold a WAAC/QMAAC Centenary Dinner for WRAC Association members.

The last WAAC veteran, Ivy Lillian Campany (née Dixon), died on 19 December 2008, aged 107. The work of the WRAC Association, historians and family history researchers will ensure that the women of the WAAC continue to be remembered.

Notes

Introduction

1. Edith Barton and Marguerite Cody, *Eve In Khaki* (London, Edinburgh, New York: Thomas Nelson and Sons Ltd, 1918).
2. Colonel Julia Cowper, *A Short History of the Queen Mary's Army Auxiliary Corps* (Aldershot: Women's Royal Army Corps Association, 1967).
3. Shelford Bidwell, *The Women's Royal Army Corps* (London: Leo Cooper Ltd, 1977).
4. Roy Terry, *Women in Khaki: The Story of the British Woman Soldier* (London: Columbus Books, 1988).

Chapter 1: Establishment

1. The National Archives (TNA), Cabinet (CAB) 17/156, *Manpower Distribution Board: Third Report of the Manpower Distribution Board*, 09 November 1916.
2. TNA, War Office (WO) 32/5251, *Letter from Haig to War Office Secretary*, 10 December 1916.
3. Ibid., *Letter from E. Geddes, Director General of Transport to Adjutant General, GHQ*, 18 December 1916.
4. TNA, WO 162/30, *Sir George Newman: Report of the Women's Services Committee*, 14 December 1916.
5. Ibid., 12.
6. Imperial War Museum (IWM), Women's Work Collection (WWC), Army 3 9/3, *Minutes of the Conference on the Organisation of Women Employed by the Army (in connection with compulsory service)*, 05 January 1917. IWM Library and Research Room Services.
7. Ibid.
8. Ibid.
9. IWM, WWC, Army 3 9/4, *Short note on Conference on the Organisation of Women Employed by the Army (in connection with compulsory service)*, 10 January 1917 and IWM, WWC, Army 3 9/5, *Minutes of Meeting on the Employment of Women in the Army*, 15 January 1917. IWM Library and Research Room Services.
10. TNA, WO 32/5251, *Letter from Haig to War Office Secretary*, 12 January 1917.
11. IWM, WWC, Army 3 1/9, *Principal Commandant VADS France Rachel Crowdy: Memorandum re Women's Service with the Army (revised copy)*, 10 January 1917. IWM Library and Research Room Services.

12. Ibid.
13. TNA, WO 32/5093, *Lieutenant General H.M. Lawson: The Number and Physical Categories of Men Employed Out of the Fighting Area in France*, 16 January 1917, 3.
14. Ibid., 4.
15. TNA, WO 32/5093, *Letter from Haig to War Office Secretary*, 25 February 1917.
16. IWM, WWC, Army 3 6/2, *Minute to AG re Women's Army Service Dept*, 15 January 1917. IWM Library and Research Room Services.
17. TNA, Ministry of National Service (NATS) 1/1271, *Letter from the Women's Interest Committee Secretary, National Union of Women Suffrage Societies to Lord Derby*, 26 January 1917.
18. IWM, WWC, Army 3 6/3, *Minute to Lord Derby re Conference for Women*, 30 January 1917. IWM Library and Research Room Services.
19. Ibid.
20. Ibid.
21. Ibid.
22. IWM, WWC, Army 3 2/15, *Katharine Furse: Third Draft for Organisation of Women's Army Corps*, 01 and 05 February 1917. IWM Library and Research Room Services.
23. Ibid.
24. IWM, WWC, Army 3 4/3, *DGT GHQ to Adjutant General*, 04 February 1917. IWM Library and Research Room Services.
25. IWM, WWC, Army 12/5, *Interview with Mrs Chalmers Watson, Edinburgh, Q.M.A.A.C. Account of First Years Work*, 09 June 1918. IWM Library and Research Room Services.
26. IWM, WWC, Army 3 9/6, *Minutes of Women's Conference*, 06 February 1917. IWM Library and Research Room Services.
27. IWM, WWC, Army 12/5, *Interview with Mrs Chalmers Watson*. IWM Library and Research Room Services.
28. Ibid.
29. Ibid.
30. Helen Gwynne-Vaughan, *Service with the Army* (London: Hutchinson, 1942).
31. Gwynne-Vaughan, *Service with the Army*, 13. Reproduced by courtesy of Birkbeck College, University of London.
32. Shelford Bidwell, Julia Cowper, Roy Terry.
33. IWM, WWC, Army 3 12/8, *Letter from Helen Gwynne-Vaughan to Mona Chalmers Watson*, 10 February 1918. IWM Library and Research Room Services. Reproduced by courtesy of Birkbeck College, University of London.
34. IWM, WWC, Army 3 10/2, *Diary of Mrs Gwynne-Vaughan re Visit to France: Memo on Administration of WAAC Army*, 25 February 1917 – 04 March 1917. IWM Library and Research Room Services.
35. Gwynne-Vaughan, *Service with the Army*, 14.
36. TNA, WO 32/5093, *Letter from Haig to War Office Secretary*, 25 February 1917.
37. TNA, WO 32/5251, *Letter on behalf of the Postmaster General to the War Office Secretary*, 03 March 1917.

38. TNA, WO 32/5093, *Letter from Haig to War Office Secretary*, 11 March 1917.

39. Ibid.

40. TNA, NATS 1/1300, *War Office: Army Council Instruction No 537 of 1917*, 28 March 1917.

41. Fryniwyd Tennyson Jesse, *The Sword of Deborah* (New York: George H. Doran, 1919), 61. Written in March 1918 but not published until 1919.

42. TNA, WO 32/5093, *Letter from Haig to War Office Secretary*, 25 February 1917.

43. TNA, WO 32/5252, *Memo from Mrs Chalmers Watson and Mrs Gwynne-Vaughan to Lieutenant Colonel Leigh Wood*, March 1917.

44. National Army Museum (NAM), 9401-253-2066, *Papers of Dame Helen Gwynne-Vaughan, Diary of Dame Helen Gwynne-Vaughan*, 21 March 1917–28 April 1918.

45. Ibid.

46. Ibid. Reproduced by courtesy of Birkbeck College, University of London.

47. TNA, WO 32/5252, *Letter from Adjutant General, GHQ, France to War Office*, 12 April 1917.

48. NAM, 9401-253-2066, *Diary of Dame Helen Gwynne-Vaughan*.

49. The War Office, *The Army Act, 1881, and Certain Other Statutes Relating to the Army. Together with Rules of Procedure, 1881, and Rules for Summary Punishment* (London: HMSO), 1881.

50. NAM, 9401-253-2066. *Diary of Dame Helen Gwynne-Vaughan*. Reproduced by courtesy of Birkbeck College, University of London.

51. IWM, WWC, Army 3 8/5, *Minute Sheets, Women's Army Auxiliary Corps Status of Precis of Conference, Macready to H. Forster*, May 1917. IWM Library and Research Room Services.

52. Ibid., *Various memos between Director of Organisation, Director of Financial Services and AG*, 14 May 1917 to 22 May 1917.

53. IWM, WWC, Army 3 8/6, *Minutes of Conference held with Secretary of State*, 25 May 1917. IWM Library and Research Room Services.

54. Gwynne-Vaughan records in *Service with the Army* that the re-drafting took place on 01 June 1917 but *General Instructions No 1* were issued on 01 June 1917.

55. TNA, WO 95/84, *War Diary of the Chief Controller, Queen Mary's Army Auxiliary Corps*, March 1917 – October 1919.

56. Gwynne-Vaughan, *Service with the Army*, 39.

57. TNA, WO 95/84, *Women's Army Auxiliary Corps in France, Standing Orders by H.C.I. Gwynne-Vaughan, Chief Controller*, June 1917, para.1.

Chapter 2: Preparation

1. The National Archives (TNA), Ministry of National Service (NATS) 1/1300, *Draft letter from War Office to various government departments*, 05 March 1917.

2. Imperial War Museum (IWM), Women's Work Collection (WWC), Army 3 7/2, *Letter from Arthur Collins, National Service Department General Secretary to War Office Secretary*, 05 March 1917. IWM Library and Research Room Services.

3. TNA, NATS 1/1300, *Memorandum of interview between Col. Leigh-Wood, Mrs Chalmers Watson and Miss Clapham, in connection with recruiting of women for the Women's Army Auxiliary Corps*, 05 March 1917.

4. IWM, WWC, Army 3 7/4, *Letter from AG11 to General Officer Commanding-in-Chief Eastern Command and all other commands*, 15 March 1917. IWM Library and Research Room Services.

5. TNA, NATS 1/1300, cited in *Letter from Director, Women's Section to General Geddes*, 20 April 1917.

6. TNA, NATS 1/1286, *Women's Army Auxiliary Corps: publicity and general correspondence*, 1917 and TNA NATS 1/300, *Recruitment of Women: early history of Women's Army Auxiliary Corps*, 1917.

7. Elsie Cooper, IWM Sound Archive, Cat No 3137, copyright BBC.

8. TNA, NATS 1/1286, *Memo drafted (by unknown) for the benefit of public speakers*, 16 July 1917.

9. National Army Museum (NAM), 9401-253-1797–1, *Papers of Dame Helen Gwynne-Vaughan, Memoir of Dame Helen Gwynne-Vaughan*, undated.

10. Ibid. Reproduced by courtesy of Birkbeck College, University of London.

11. Ibid.

12. Ruby Adelina Ord, IWM Sound Archive, Cat No 44, copyright IWM.

13. Agnes Anderson, ed. *"Johnnie" of QMAAC* (London: Heath Cranton, 1920), 16.

14. Elsie Cooper, IWM Sound Archive, Cat No 3137, copyright BBC.

15. TNA, War Office (WO) 32/5251, *Statement of the Services form*, undated.

16. TNA, WO 95/84, *War Diary of GHQ 1st Echelon attached to Director of Ordnance Service, Queen Mary's Army Auxiliary Corps*, July 1917 – December 1918.

17. TNA, WO 95/84, *War Diary of GHQ 2nd Echelon, Queen Mary's Army Auxiliary Corps*, November 1917 – March 1919.

18. TNA, WO 32/5093, *Lieutenant General H.M. Lawson: The Number and Physical Categories of Men Employed Out of the Fighting Area in France*, 16 January 1917, 16.

19. TNA, WO 32/5252, *Proposals regarding uniform and badges to be worn by women holding positions equivalent to commissioned rank*, 1917.

20. Helen Gwynne-Vaughan, *Service with the Army* (London: Hutchinson, 1942), 18. Reproduced by courtesy of Birkbeck College, University of London.

21. Anderson, *"Johnnie" of QMAAC*, 23.

22. Ruby Adelina Ord, IWM Sound Archive, Cat No 44, copyright IWM.

23. TNA, WO 32/5252, *Proposals regarding uniform and badges*, 1917.

24. Ruby Adelina Ord, IWM Sound Archive, Cat No 44, copyright IWM.

25. NAM, 9401-253-1796, *Letter from Dame Helen Gwynne-Vaughan to Miss Ireland*, 18 January 1941. Reproduced by courtesy of Birkbeck College, University of London.

26. TNA, WO 95/84, *The Employment of the Women's Army Auxiliary Corps with the British Armies in France, General Instructions No 1*, 01 June 1917.

27. TNA, WO 95/84, *War Diary of GHQ 1st Echelon*.

28. Emily Maud Victoria Rumbold, IWM Sound Archive, Cat No 576, copyright IWM.

29. Fryniwyd Tennyson Jesse, *The Sword of Deborah* (New York: George H. Doran, 1919), 19. Written in March 1918 but not published until 1919.

30. *Manchester Evening News*, November 30, 1917, 5. Used by kind permission of Trinity Mirror Plc.

31. IWM, Art.IWM PST 2763, *Women of Britain Say 'Go!'*, 1915.

32. Edith Barton and Marguerite Cody, *Eve In Khaki* (London, Edinburgh, New York: Thomas Nelson and Sons Ltd, 1918), 5.

33. Radclyffe Hall, *The Well of Loneliness* (London: Jonathan Cape, 1928).

34. TNA, WO 95/84, *War Diary of the DGT, GHQ and GHQ Club Units, Queen Mary's Army Auxiliary Corps*, September 1917 – November 1918.

35. *Birmingham Daily Post*, November 19, 1917, 7. Used by kind permission of Trinity Mirror Plc.

36. *Liverpool Daily Post and Mercury*, November 21, 1917, 7. Used by kind permission of Trinity Mirror Plc.

37. *Aberdeen Daily Journal*, November 24, 1917, 4. Used by kind permission of *The Press and Journal* and DC Thomson & Co Ltd.

38. Ruby Adelina Ord, IWM Sound Archive, Cat No 44, copyright IWM.

39. Annie May Martin, IWM Sound Archive, Cat No 42, copyright IWM.

40. Mabel Dymond Peel, *The Story of the Hush-Waacs* (Newcastle-under-Lyme: Mandley and Unett, 1921), 3.

41. Annie May Martin, IWM Sound Archive, Cat No 42, copyright IWM.

42. Amy Winifred Hall, IWM Sound Archive, Cat No 12307, copyright IWM.

43. Ruby Adelina Ord, IWM Sound Archive, Cat No 44, copyright IWM.

44. Elsie Cooper, IWM Sound Archive, Cat No 3137, copyright BBC.

45. TNA, WO 162/42, *Letter from Miss Durham, Ministry of Labour, Employment Dept., H Section to AG11 Devonshire House*, 25 February 1918.

46. The Department of National Service became the Ministry of National Service in March 1917. The Ministry is referred to variously as the Ministry for National Service, the Department of National Service and the National Service Department according to the way it is recorded in the primary sources.

47. TNA, NATS 1/1286, *National Service Department, Internal Memo*, 27 June 1917.

48. Ibid., *Various letters and memos*, 18 June 1917 to 23 June 1917.

49. TNA, NATS 1/1300, *War Office: Army Council Instruction No 537 of 1917*, 28 March 1917, para. 3 and *Army Council Instruction No. 1069 of 1917*, 07 July 1917, para. 10.

50. TNA, WO 32/5251, *Letter on behalf of the Postmaster General to the War Office Secretary*, 09 May 1917.

51. TNA, NATS 1/1302, *Memo from Miss Clapham to Miss Markham*, 13 July 1917.

52. TNA, NATS 1/1271, *Clerical candidates for Women's Army Auxiliary Corps*, 14 July 1917.

53. TNA, WO 32/5093, *Note on file*, 24 August 1917.

54. TNA, NATS 1/1302, *Letter from Deputy Director, Women's Section to Colonel Scovell, War Office*, 17 May 1917.

55. IWM, WWC, Army 3 12/3, *History of the Corps*, 14 May 1918. IWM Library and Research Room Services.
56. TNA, WO 162/42, *Minutes of meeting of Interdepartmental Committee*, 29 October 1917.
57. Auckland Geddes was appointed to the Most Honourable Order of the Bath in the King's Birthday Honours list in June 1917.
58. *Motherwell Times*, October 12, 1917, 5. Used by kind permission of the *Motherwell Times* and Johnston Press Plc.
59. *Birmingham Daily Post*, December 20, 1917, 9. Used by kind permission of Trinity Mirror Plc.
60. TNA, NATS 1/1271, *Letter from Sir Auckland Geddes to G.H. Roberts*, 05 February 1918.
61. TNA, NATS 1/1282, *Memo titled Shortage Overseas*, 18 June 1918.
62. IWM, E.J. 1027, *Old Comrades Association Gazette* 16, no. 44 (April 1936): 1.
63. Ibid., *Old Comrades Association Gazette* 16, no. 44 (April 1936): 1.

Chapter 3: Daily Life

1. The National Archives (TNA), War Office (WO) 95/84, *War Diary of the Chief Controller, Queen Mary's Army Auxiliary Corps*, March 1917 – October 1919.
2. Ibid.
3. Ibid.
4. Last Woman to Leave the *Warilda*. *The Times* (London, England), Wednesday, Aug 07, 1918; pg. 3; Issue 41862. © Times Newspapers Ltd. News UK & Ireland Limited, 1918.
5. Charlotte Kathleen Bottomley, Imperial War Museum (IWM) Sound Archive, Cat No 172, copyright IWM.
6. IWM Documents.11301, *Private Papers of the Hon Dorothy F. Pickford OBE*. Used by kind permission of J. Bailey.
7. Charlotte Kathleen Bottomley, IWM Sound Archive, Cat No 172, copyright IWM.
8. Annie May Martin, IWM Sound Archive, Cat No 42, copyright IWM.
9. Agnes Anderson, ed. *"Johnnie" of QMAAC* (London: Heath Cranton, 1920), 28.
10. Ibid., 70.
11. TNA, WO 95/84, *War Diary of the Area Controller, Women's Army Auxiliary Corps, Abbeville Area*, 05 August 1917 – 31 August 1917.
12. Fryniwyd Tennyson Jesse, *The Sword of Deborah* (New York: George H. Doran, 1919), 69. Written in March 1918 but not published until 1919.
13. IWM, Art.IWM ART 2904, Beatrice Lithiby: *The Workers' Quarters, Queen Mary's Army Auxiliary Corps: Queen Elizabeth Camp, Vendroux*.
14. Ruby Adelina Ord, IWM Sound Archive, Cat No 44, copyright IWM.
15. Mabel Dymond Peel, *The Story of the Hush-Waacs* (Newcastle-under-Lyme: Mandley and Unett, 1921), 17.
16. Anderson, *"Johnnie" of QMAAC*, 30.
17. Ruby Adelina Ord, IWM Sound Archive, Cat No 44, copyright IWM.

18. Charlotte Kathleen Bottomley, IWM Sound Archive, Cat No 172, copyright IWM.
19. TNA, Ministry of National Service (NATS) 1/1300, *War Office: Army Council Instruction No 613 of 1917*, 13 April 1917, para. 5.
20. Anderson, *"Johnnie" of QMAAC*, 85.
21. TNA, WO 95/84, *War Diary of GHQ 2nd Echelon, Queen Mary's Army Auxiliary Corps*, November 1917 – March 1919.
22. IWM Documents.11301, *Private Papers of the Hon Dorothy F. Pickford OBE*. Used by kind permission of J. Bailey.
23. TNA, WO 95/84, *War Diary of the Chief Controller*.
24. Charlotte Kathleen Bottomley, IWM Sound Archive, Cat No 172, copyright IWM.
25. Edith Barton and Marguerite Cody, *Eve In Khaki* (London, Edinburgh, New York: Thomas Nelson and Sons Ltd, 1918), 130.
26. Charlotte Kathleen Bottomley, IWM Sound Archive, Cat No 172, copyright IWM.
27. TNA, Cabinet Office (CAB) 24/46/30, *Women's Army Auxiliary Corps. Report of Commission of Enquiry forwarded by Minister of Labour*, 20 March 1918, 3.
28. Ruby Adelina Ord, IWM Sound Archive, Cat No 44, copyright IWM.
29. Charlotte Kathleen Bottomley, IWM Sound Archive, Cat No 172, copyright IWM.
30. Anderson, *"Johnnie" of QMAAC*, 75.
31. Ibid., 94.
32. Ibid.
33. Helen Gwynne-Vaughan, *Service with the Army* (London: Hutchinson, 1942), 26. Reproduced by courtesy of Birkbeck College, University of London.
34. Nora Barker, IWM Sound Archive, Cat No 9731, copyright IWM.
35. Emily Maud Victoria Rumbold, IWM Sound Archive, Cat No 576, copyright IWM.
36. Ruby Adelina Ord, IWM Sound Archive, Cat No 44, copyright IWM.
37. Peel, *The Story of the Hush-Waacs*, 14.
38. TNA, CAB 24/46/30, *Report of Commission of Enquiry*, 3.
39. IWM Documents.11301, *Private Papers of the Hon Dorothy F. Pickford OBE*. Used by kind permission of J. Bailey.
40. Elsie Cooper, IWM Sound Archive, Cat No 3137, copyright BBC.
41. Ibid.
42. Ibid.
43. TNA, WO 95/84, *War Diary of GHQ 1st Echelon attached to Director of Ordnance Service, Queen Mary's Army Auxiliary Corps*, July 1917 – December 1918.
44. *Hastings and St. Leonards Observer*, March 09, 1918, 6. Used by kind permission of the *Hastings and St. Leonards Observer* and Johnston Press Plc.
45. Ruby Adelina Ord, IWM Sound Archive, Cat No 44, copyright IWM.
46. Ibid.
47. Peel, *The Story of the Hush-Waacs*, 20.
48. National Army Museum (NAM), 9401-253-2066, *Papers of Dame Helen Gwynne-Vaughan, Diary of Dame Helen Gwynne-Vaughan*, 21 March 1917–28 April 1918.
49. IWM, E.J. 1027, *Old Comrades Association Gazette* 6, no. 5 (November 1925): 4. Used by kind permission of the Women's Royal Army Corps (WRAC) Association.

50. Ruby Adelina Ord, IWM Sound Archive, Cat No 44, copyright IWM.
51. TNA, CAB 24/46/30, *Report of Commission of Enquiry*, 2.
52. TNA, WO 95/84, *War Diary of the DGT, GHQ and GHQ Club Units, Queen Mary's Army Auxiliary Corps*, September 1917 – November 1918.
53. TNA, WO 95/84, *Women's Army Auxiliary Corps in France, Standing Orders by H.C.I. Gwynne-Vaughan, Chief Controller*, June 1917, para. 14.
54. Jesse, *The Sword of Deborah*, 53.
55. Anderson, *"Johnnie" of QMAAC*, 97.
56. Ruby Adelina Ord, IWM Sound Archive, Cat No 44, copyright IWM.
57. IWM Documents.11301, *Private Papers of the Hon Dorothy F. Pickford OBE*. Used by kind permission of J. Bailey.
58. NAM, 9811-16, *Papers on the connection of Queen Mary with the Queen Mary's Army Auxiliary Corps, 1918–1922, Answers to a series of questions received from the Queen*, 28 May 1918.
59. Ibid.
60. TNA, NATS 1/1300, *War Office: Army Council Instruction No. 1069 of 1917*, 07 July 1917, para. 24.
61. Lilias is the correct spelling.
62. TNA, WO 95/84, *War Diary of GHQ 1st Echelon*.

Chapter 4: Work

1. The War Office, *Regulations for the Queen Mary's Army Auxiliary Corps 1918* (London: HMSO, 1918), 8–9.
2. The National Archives (TNA), War Office (WO) 32/5093, *Lieutenant General H.M. Lawson: The Number and Physical Categories of Men Employed Out of the Fighting Area in France*, 16 January 1917, 12 and *Letter from Haig to War Office Secretary*, 11 March 1917.
3. National Army Museum (NAM), 9401-253-2066, *Papers of Dame Helen Gwynne-Vaughan, Diary of Dame Helen Gwynne-Vaughan*, 21 March 1917–28 April 1918.
4. Imperial War Museum (IWM), E.J. 1027, *Old Comrades Association Gazette* 16, no. 44 (April 1936): 2.
5. TNA, WO 32/5093, *Lieutenant General H.M. Lawson*, 16.
6. Edith Barton and Marguerite Cody, *Eve In Khaki* (London, Edinburgh, New York: Thomas Nelson and Sons Ltd, 1918), 35.
7. Elsie Cooper, IWM Sound Archive, Cat No 3137, copyright BBC.
8. Dolly Shepherd, IWM Sound Archive, Cat No 579, copyright IWM.
9. Ibid.
10. Annie May Martin, IWM Sound Archive, Cat No 42, copyright IWM.
11. Agnes Anderson, ed. *"Johnnie" of QMAAC* (London: Heath Cranton, 1920), 19.
12. Ibid., 17.
13. Ibid., 30.
14. Barton and Cody, *Eve In Khaki*, 148.

15. Mabel Dymond Peel, *The Story of the Hush-Waacs* (Newcastle-under-Lyme: Mandley and Unett, 1921), 7.

16. Ibid., 9.

17. Ibid., 13.

18. Helen Gwynne-Vaughan, *Service with the Army* (London: Hutchinson, 1942), 35. Reproduced by courtesy of Birkbeck College, University of London.

19. Anon, IWM Sound Archive, Cat No 7448, copyright Southampton Museums.

20. Barton and Cody, *Eve In Khaki*, 175.

21. TNA, Ministry of National Service (NATS) 1/1300, *Memo from Miss Clapham to Miss Markham*, 23 April 1917.

22. TNA, WO 95/84, *War Diary of the Chief Controller, Queen Mary's Army Auxiliary Corps*, March 1917 – October 1919.

23. TNA, NATS 1/1300, *Letter from Director of Recruiting, War Office to Director General, National Service (Women's Section)*, 03 July 1917.

24. Nora Barker, IWM Sound Archive, Cat No 9731, copyright IWM.

25. Ibid.

26. *Illustrated London News*, March 02, 1918, 261.

27. Fryniwyd Tennyson Jesse, *The Sword of Deborah* (New York: George H. Doran, 1919), 61. Written in March 1918 but not published until 1919.

28. TNA, WO 162/42, *Minutes of the conference held on Monday 10 June between representatives of the QMAAC, WRNS, and Ministry of Labour, Employment Department*, 10 June 1918.

29. Ibid.

30. Charlotte Kathleen Bottomley, IWM Sound Archive, Cat No 172, copyright IWM.

31. Annie May Martin, IWM Sound Archive, Cat No 42, copyright IWM.

32. Roy Terry, *Women In Khaki: the Story of the British Woman Soldier* (London: Columbus Books, 1988), 78 and Colonel Julia Cowper, *A Short History of the Queen Mary's Army Auxiliary Corps* (Aldershot: Women's Royal Army Corps Association, 1967), 60.

33. TNA, WO 162/52, *David L. Stone, Colonel, General Staff Commanding Headquarters United States Troops, Bourges (Cher) France, General Orders No 46*, June 27 1919.

34. Ibid., *Telegraph from Adjutant General Davis AEF to Florence* Leach, QMAAC Chief Controller, 27 June 1919.

35. NAM, 9811-6, *Three groups of papers relating to the Queen Mary's Army Auxiliary Corps (QMAAC), Telegram from Adjutant General HAEF to Colonel Stone*, 29 June 1919.

36. TNA, WO 162/52, *Letter from Florence Leach to Colonel David L. Stone, Commanding Headquarters, United States Troops, Bourges (Cher) France*, 03 July 1919.

37. TNA, Air Force (AIR) 10/18, *Voluntary transfer of officers and members of the Women's Royal Naval Service, the Women's Army Auxiliary Corps and the Women's Legion Motor Drivers to the Women's RAF*, 1918.

38. Barton and Cody, *Eve In Khaki*, 104.

39. TNA, WO 162/40, *War Office: Co-ordinating Conference of Women's Corps, Leave for members from overseas,* 30 August 1918.
40. TNA, NATS 1/1300, *War Office: Army Council Instruction No 537 of 1917,* 28 March 1917, para. 3.
41. TNA, NATS 1/1300, *War Office: Army Council Instruction No. 1069 of 1917,* 07 July 1917, para. 10.
42. Ibid.
43. TNA, NATS 1/1286, *Letter from the Army Council to the Treasury Secretary,* 01 December 1918.
44. The War Office, *Regulations for the Queen Mary's Army Auxiliary Corps 1918,* 33–36.
45. Ibid., 34–35.
46. TNA, WO 162/40, *Minutes of the fourth meeting of the Co-ordinating Conference on Women's Corps,* 10 June 1918.
47. The War Office, *Regulations for the Queen Mary's Army Auxiliary Corps 1918,* 46.
48. Emily Maud Victoria Rumbold, IWM Sound Archive, Cat No 576, copyright IWM.
49. Anderson, *"Johnnie" of QMAAC,* 35.
50. TNA, Treasury (T) 1/12239, *Letter from the War Office to the Treasury Secretary,* 30 September 1918.
51. Ibid., *War Office file on improvements in rates of pay for QMAAC Administrators,* 30 October 1918.
52. Ibid., *Letter from the War Office to the Treasury Secretary,* 09 December 1918.
53. Ibid., *Treasury: internal memo from A.P. Waterfield,* 25 March 1919.
54. Ibid., *Letter from the Treasury to the War Office Secretary,* 11 April 1919.

Chapter 5: Controversy

1. Men for the Army. *The Times* (London, England), Tuesday, Nov 13, 1917; pg. 3; Issue 41634. © Times Newspapers Ltd. News UK & Ireland Limited, 1917.
2. Imperial War Museum (IWM) Documents.129, *Private Papers of R. Cude MM,* 1922.
3. Charlotte Kathleen Bottomley, IWM Sound Archive, Cat No 172, copyright IWM.
4. Annie May Martin, IWM Sound Archive, Cat No 42, copyright IWM.
5. The National Archives (TNA), War Office (WO) 162/42, *Minutes of the War Office Conference,* 10 December 1917.
6. Ibid., *Letter from Miss Durham, Ministry of Labour, Employment Dept. to AG11,* 25 February 1918.
7. Charlotte Kathleen Bottomley, IWM Sound Archive, Cat No 172, copyright IWM.
8. Nora Barker, IWM Sound Archive, Cat No 9731, copyright IWM.
9. The Church in War. *The Times* (London, England), Wednesday, Feb 06, 1918; pg. 3; Issue 41706. © Times Newspapers Ltd. News UK & Ireland Limited, 1918.
10. *Edinburgh Evening News,* February 06, 1918, 4.
11. Social Impurity. *The Times* (London, England), Thursday, Feb 07, 1918; pg. 3; Issue 41707. © Times Newspapers Ltd. News UK & Ireland Limited, 1918.

12. IWM, Women's Work Collection (WWC), Army 3 12/7, *Farewell Order to the WAAC*, undated. IWM Library and Research Room Services.
13. *Liverpool Echo*, February 09, 1918, 3. Used by kind permission of Trinity Mirror Plc.
14. *Birmingham Daily Post*, February 12, 1918, 3. Used by kind permission of Trinity Mirror Plc.
15. TNA, WO 95/84, *War Diary of the Chief Controller, Queen Mary's Army Auxiliary Corps*, March 1917 – October 1919.
16. IWM Documents.11301, *Private Papers of the Hon Dorothy F. Pickford OBE*. Used by kind permission of J. Bailey.
17. Fryniwyd Tennyson Jesse, *The Sword of Deborah* (New York: George H. Doran, 1919). Written in March 1918 but not published until 1919.
18. Jesse, *The Sword of Deborah*, 52.
19. TNA, Cabinet Office (CAB) 24/46/30, *Women's Army Auxiliary Corps. Report of Commission of Enquiry forwarded by Minister of Labour*, 20 March 1918, 1.
20. Ibid., 2.
21. Ibid.
22. Ibid., 4.
23. Ibid.
24. Ibid., 6–7.
25. TNA, WO 162/40, *Minutes of the ninth meeting of the Co-ordinating Conference on Women's Corps*, 03 August 1918.
26. TNA, CAB 24/46/30, *Report of Commission of Enquiry*, 2.
27. Official figures cited in Arthur Marwick, *Women at War, 1914–1918* (London: Fontana, 1977), 169.
28. TNA, Ministry of National Service (NATS) 1/1300, *Letter from Ministry of National Service, General Secretary to War Office, Recruiting Director*, 14 June 1917.
29. Ruby Adelina Ord, IWM Sound Archive, Cat No 44, copyright IWM.

Chapter 6: Danger
1. Mabel Dymond Peel, *The Story of the Hush-Waacs* (Newcastle-under-Lyme: Mandley and Unett, 1921), 20.
2. Imperial War Museum (IWM), E.J. 1027, *Old Comrades Association Gazette* 18, no. 4 (April 1938): 2. Used by kind permission of the Women's Royal Army Corps (WRAC) Association.
3. Elsie Cooper, IWM Sound Archive, Cat No 3137, copyright BBC.
4. Agnes Anderson, ed. *"Johnnie" of QMAAC* (London: Heath Cranton, 1920), 88.
5. The National Archives (TNA), War Office (WO) 95/84, *War Diary of the Chief Controller, Queen Mary's Army Auxiliary Corps*, March 1917 – October 1919.
6. Ibid., *War Diary of the Area Controller, Women's Army Auxiliary Corps, Abbeville Area*, 05 August 1917 – 31 August 1917.
7. Ibid., *War Diary of the Chief Controller*.
8. Anderson, *"Johnnie" of QMAAC*, 101.
9. Charlotte Kathleen Bottomley, IWM Sound Archive, Cat No 172, copyright IWM.

10. Ibid.
11. Cited in The War Office, *Statistics of the Military Effort of the British Empire during the Great War, 1914–20* (London: HMSO, 1922), 205.
12. National Army Museum (NAM), 9811-16, *Papers on the connection of Queen Mary with the Queen Mary's Army Auxiliary Corps, 1918–1922, Special Order from Chief Controller to Area Controller*, 11 April 1918.
13. As stated in the Introduction, in most cases throughout this book, the Corps is referred to as the WAAC rather than the QMAAC.
14. TNA, WO 95/84, *War Diary of GHQ 1st Echelon attached to Director of Ordnance Service, Queen Mary's Army Auxiliary Corps*, July 1917 – December 1918.
15. NAM, 9811-16, *Answers to a series of questions received from the Queen*, 28 May 1918.
16. TNA, WO 95/84, *War Diary of the Chief Controller*.
17. Charlotte Kathleen Bottomley, IWM Sound Archive, Cat No 172, copyright IWM.
18. Ibid.
19. Commonwealth War Graves Commission (CWGC), *Women's Army Auxiliary Corps and Queen Mary's Army Auxiliary Corps, Commonwealth War Graves Commission Casualty Report 1916–1921*.
20. Charlotte Kathleen Bottomley, IWM Sound Archive, Cat No 172, copyright IWM.
21. Helen Gwynne-Vaughan, *Service with the Army* (London: Hutchinson, 1942), 57. Reproduced by courtesy of Birkbeck College, University of London.
22. TNA, WO 95/84, *War Diary of the Chief Controller*.
23. CWGC, *WAAC and QMAAC CWGC Casualty Report 1916–1921*.
24. Charlotte Kathleen Bottomley, IWM Sound Archive, Cat No 172, copyright IWM.
25. Ibid.
26. TNA, WO 95/84, *War Diary of the Chief Controller*.
27. Gwynne-Vaughan, *Service with the Army*, 57.
28. *Yorkshire Evening Post*, June 01, 1918, 5. Used by kind permission of the *Yorkshire Evening Post* and Johnston Press Plc.
29. *Evening Telegraph and Post, Dundee*, June 05, 1918, 1. Used by kind permission of the *Dundee Evening Telegraph* and DC Thomson & Co Ltd.
30. Charlotte Kathleen Bottomley, IWM Sound Archive, Cat No 172, copyright IWM.
31. TNA, WO 95/84, *War Diary of the Area Controller, Abbeville Area*.
32. IWM, E.J. 1027, *Old Comrades Association Gazette* 16, no. 44 (April 1936): 2.
33. TNA, WO 95/84, *War Diary of the Area Controller, Abbeville Area*.
34. CWGC, *WAAC and QMAAC CWGC Casualty Report 1916–1921*.
35. TNA, WO 95/84, *War Diary of the Area Controller, Abbeville Area*.
36. Ibid., *War Diary of the Chief Controller*.

Chapter 7: Disbandment

1. The National Archives (TNA), War Office (WO) 95/84, *War Diary of the Chief Controller, Queen Mary's Army Auxiliary Corps*, March 1917 – October 1919.
2. Ibid., *War Diary of GHQ 1st Echelon attached to Director of Ordnance Service, Queen Mary's Army Auxiliary Corps*, July 1917 – December 1918.

3. Ruby Adelina Ord, Imperial War Museum (IWM) Sound Archive, Cat No 44, copyright IWM.

4. Annie May Martin, IWM Sound Archive, Cat No 42, copyright IWM.

5. Agnes Anderson, ed. *"Johnnie" of QMAAC* (London: Heath Cranton, 1920), 155.

6. Mabel Colebrooke Carey, *Princess Mary: A Biography* (London: Nisbet & Co. Ltd, 1922), 121. Used by kind permission of James Clarke & Co Ltd.

7. Anderson, *"Johnnie" of QMAAC*, 154.

8. Charlotte Kathleen Bottomley, IWM Sound Archive, Cat No 172, copyright IWM.

9. IWM, E.J. 1027, *Old Comrades Association Gazette* (March – April 1946): 5. Used by kind permission of the Women's Royal Army Corps (WRAC) Association.

10. TNA, WO 95/84, *War Diary of GHQ 2nd Echelon, Queen Mary's Army Auxiliary Corps*, November 1917 – March 1919.

11. Emily Maud Victoria Rumbold, IWM Sound Archive, Cat No 576, copyright IWM.

12. Ibid.

13. Anderson, *"Johnnie" of QMAAC*, 153.

14. Emily Maud Victoria Rumbold, IWM Sound Archive, Cat No 576, copyright IWM.

15. TNA, WO 33/3284, *War Office: Report of the Women War Workers Resettlement Committee*, 18 November 1918.

16. TNA, Treasury (T) 1/12299, *Letter from the War Office Secretary to the Treasury Secretary*, 20 February 1919.

17. Ibid., *War Office: Position as regards demobilisation of Women's Corps*, 20 February 1919.

18. Emily Maud Victoria Rumbold, IWM Sound Archive, Cat No 576, copyright IWM.

19. The Women's Services. *The Times* (London, England), Thursday, Aug 28, 1919; pg. 13; Issue 42190. © Times Newspapers Ltd. News UK & Ireland Limited, 1919.

20. TNA, WO 162/53, *Letter from Director General of Mobilisation to War Cabinet Secretary, Coordination of Demobilisation Section*, 21 October 1919.

21. IWM, Women's Work Collection (WWC), Army 3 12/16, *Chief Controller Davy, QMAAC Order*, 01 December 1919. IWM Library and Research Room Services.

22. The War Office, *Army Council Order 5*, 16 January 1920.

23. IWM, E.J. 1027, *Old Comrades Association Gazette*, no. 8 (February 1921): 1. Used by kind permission of the WRAC Association.

24. Ibid., *Old Comrades Association Gazette 2*, no. 7 (January 1922): 2.

25. Ibid. Used by kind permission of the WRAC Association.

26. Ibid.

27. Ibid., *Old Comrades Association Gazette*, no. 9 (March 1921): 1.

28. Annie May Martin, IWM Sound Archive, Cat No 42, copyright IWM.

29. Ruby Adelina Ord, IWM Sound Archive, Cat No 44, copyright IWM.

30. IWM, E.J. 1027, *Old Comrades Association Gazette*, no.6 (December 1920): 6.

31. Ethel Tweedie, (Mrs Alec Tweedie), *Women and Soldiers* (London: John Lane, 1918), 2.

32. *Daily Mirror*, November 11, 1918, 1.

33. Annie May Martin, IWM Sound Archive, Cat No 42, copyright IWM.

34. Ruby Adelina Ord, IWM Sound Archive, Cat No 44, copyright IWM.
35. Ibid.
36. *Daily Mirror*, December 10, 1918, 10. Used by kind permission of Trinity Mirror Plc.
37. TNA, T 1/12299, *Treasury: Demobilisation benefits of Women's Corps*, 17 January 1919.
38. IWM, E.J. 1027, *Old Comrades Association Gazette*, no. 1 (July 1920): 2. Used by kind permission of the WRAC Association.
39. *The Evening Telegraph and Post, Dundee*, May 13, 1920, 4.
40. Oversea is the correct spelling but it is often referred to as Overseas.
41. TNA, WO 162/40, *Minutes of the sixteenth meeting of the Co-ordinating Conference on Women's Corps*, 14 January 1919.
42. TNA, WO 162/54, *Letter from War Services Committee Secretary to Miss Bowen, Unit Administrator, QMAAC*, 09 December 1919.
43. Ibid., *Letter from Oversea Settlement Committee Secretary to Florence Leach*, 23 August 1919.
44. IWM, E.J. 1027, *Old Comrades Association Gazette*, no. 3 (September 1920): 1.
45. Ibid., *Old Comrades Association Gazette*, no. 6 (December 1920): 2.
46. Ibid., *Old Comrades Association Gazette* 2, no. 7 (January 1922): 1.
47. TNA, T 1/12299, *Letter from the War Office to the Treasury Secretary*, 03 December 1918.
48. Ibid., *Treasury: Handwritten note within file by A.P. Waterfield*, 06 December 1918.
49. Ibid., *Memo from C. Harris (War Office) to G. Barstow (Treasury)*, 09 January 1919.
50. Ibid., *Letter from War Office to Treasury Secretary*, 17 January 1919.
51. TNA, T 1/12560, *Letter from Walthamstow Local Pensions Committee Secretary to the Minister for Pensions*, 20 October 1919.
52. *Hansard, House of Commons*, 5th Series, Vol. 122, 1 December – 12 December 1919, Oral Answers, col. 542.
53. TNA, T 1/12560, *Treasury: Internal minute of meeting between Treasury, Ministry of Pensions, WAAC, WRNS, WRAF*, 12 December 1919.
54. *Hansard, House of Commons*, 5th Series, Vol. 125, 10 February – 27 February 1920, Oral Answers, col. 1036–7.
55. TNA, T 1/12560, *Letter from A. Hore (Ministry of Pensions) to Viscount Cross (Treasury)*, 21 February 1920.
56. *Hansard*, Vol. 125, col. 1881–2.
57. TNA, T 1/12560, *Minutes of Conference held between Ministry of Pensions, Treasury, War Office, QMAAC, Admiralty and Air Ministry*, 05 March 1920.
58. TNA, Ministry of Pensions and National Insurance (PIN) 15/2448, *Letter from Edith Thompson, Assistant Chief Controller, QMAAC, to A. Hore (Ministry of Pensions)*, 08 April 1920.
59. TNA, PIN 13/3063, *Letter from E. Greenhalgh to Her Majesty the Queen*, undated but forwarded to the Ministry of Pensions on 24 July 1939.
60. Tweedie, *Women and Soldiers*, 26.

61. IWM, E.J. 1027, *Old Comrades Association Gazette* 2, no. 1 (July 1921): 1. Used by kind permission of the WRAC Association.

62. Helen Gwynne-Vaughan, *Service with the Army* (London: Hutchinson, 1942), 138. Reproduced by courtesy of Birkbeck College, University of London.

63. Gwynne-Vaughan, *Service with the Army*, 139.

Chapter 8: Memory

1. Imperial War Museum (IWM), EN1/3/SER/018, *Letter from Lady Priscilla Norman to Mona Chalmers Watson*, 13 February 1918. IWM Museum Archive.

2. Ibid., *Letter from Lady Priscilla Norman to Dame Florence Leach*, 25 April 1918.

3. IWM, EN1/3/DEA/014/9, *Letter from Agnes Conway to Dame Florence Leach*, 26 August 1918. IWM Museum Archive.

4. IWM, EN1/3/DEA/020/44, *Deaths: Other Services – Munition Workers, Miss Jeanie Watson*, 31 August 1918. IWM Museum Archive. Used by kind permission of L. McNulty. NB this letter has been filed in the Munition Workers file as *Oliphant, Fearne to IWM* (a misspelling of Jeanie Oliphant) noting that Miss Jeanie Watson's unit is unknown.

5. IWM, EN1/3/SER/018, *Letter from Lady Priscilla Norman to Dame Florence Leach*, 11 September 1918. IWM Museum Archive.

6. Ibid., *Letter from Lady Priscilla Norman to Dame Florence Leach*, 04 June 1920.

7. IWM, Documents.140, *The Record of a Journey to Photograph the British Women's Services Overseas Begun on Sunday March 2nd 1919*, 27. IWM Museum Archive.

8. Ibid., 30.

9. Ibid., 27.

10. The National Archives (TNA), War Office (WO) 95/84, *War Diary of the Chief Controller, Queen Mary's Army Auxiliary Corps*, March 1917 – October 1919.

11. Helen Gwynne-Vaughan, *Service with the Army* (London: Hutchinson, 1942), 66. Reproduced by courtesy of Birkbeck College, University of London.

12. IWM, Art.IWM ART 3048, William Orpen: *The First Chief Controller, QMAAC in France, Dame Helen Gwynne-Vaughan, CBE, DSC*, 1918.

13. IWM, EN1/3/SER/018, *Letter from WWSC to Dame Florence Leach*, 30 January 1919. IWM Museum Archive.

14. Ibid., *Letter from Lady Priscilla Norman to Dame Florence Leach*, 12 February 1919.

15. Ibid., *Letter from Dame Florence Leach to Lady Priscilla Norman*, 01 May 1919.

16. Ibid., Cited in *Letter from Lady Priscilla Norman to Dame Florence Leach*, 19 April 1919.

17. Ibid., *Letter from Lila Davy to Agnes Conway*, 11 June 1919.

18. TNA, WO 95/84, *War Diary of the Chief Controller*.

19. IWM, Art.IWM ART 3093, Austin Spare: *Queen Mary's Army Auxiliary Corps: Tending Graves at Wimereux Cemetery*.

20. IWM, Art.IWM ART 3091, Geneste Beeton: *Miss Penrose, MM, QMAAC Administrator; Superintending French labour on camouflage at Aire*.

21. Geneste Beeton was awarded the MM in April 1919 and the investiture was in June 1920.
22. Bessie Marchant, *A Transport Girl in France: A Story of the Adventures of a WAAC* (London: Blackie & Son Ltd, 1919).
23. Helen Zenna Smith, *Not So Quiet: Stepdaughters of War* (London: A.E. Marriott, 1930).
24. Helen Zenna Smith, *Not So Quiet: Stepdaughters of War* (New York: The Feminist Press, 1989), 211. Copyright 1930 by Helen Zenna Smith. Reprinted with the permission of The Permissions Company, Inc., on behalf of the Feminist Press, www.feministpress.org.
25. Smith, *Not So Quiet: Stepdaughters of War* (New York: The Feminist Press, 1989).
26. Anonymous, *The Letters of Thomasina Atkins: Private W.A.A.C. on Active Service* (New York: George H. Doran, 1918).
27. Ibid., 16.
28. Ibid., 30.
29. Agnes Anderson, ed. *"Johnnie" of QMAAC* (London: Heath Cranton, 1920).
30. Ibid., 190.
31. Edith Barton and Marguerite Cody, *Eve In Khaki* (London, Edinburgh, New York: Thomas Nelson and Sons Ltd, 1918).
32. Ibid., 182.
33. Anonymous, *WAAC: The Woman's Story of the War* (London: T. Werner Laurie Ltd, 1930).
34. IWM, E.J. 1027, *Old Comrades Association Gazette* 11, no. 10 (April 1930): 6. Used by kind permission of the Women's Royal Army Corps (WRAC) Association.
35. Richard Aldington, *Death of a Hero* (London, Chatto & Windus, 1929).
36. IWM, E.J. 1027, *Old Comrades Association Gazette* 11, no. 10 (April 1930): 1.
37. Winifred Holtby, *Letters to a Friend* (London: Collins, 1937).
38. Hull History Centre, Winifred Holtby Collection, L WH/11/11.3/01/03a.
39. Charlotte Kathleen Bottomley, IWM Sound Archive, Cat No 172, copyright IWM.
40. Vera Brittain, *Testament of Friendship: The Story of Winifred Holtby* (London: Macmillan, 1940).
41. TNA, WO 95/84, *War Diary of the Chief Controller*.
42. I. Grindlay 3617, *Ripples from the Ranks of the Q.M.A.A.C.* (London: Erskine Macdonald Ltd, 1918).
43. IWM, E.J. 1027, *Old Comrades Association Gazette*, no. 6 (December 1920): 2.
44. TNA, Board of Trade (BT) 31/27119/180619, *Memorandum and Articles of Association of the Queen Mary's Army Auxiliary Corps (Old Comrades Association) Limited*, 25 March 1922.
45. IWM, E.J. 1027, *Old Comrades Association Gazette*, no. 1 (July 1920): 2.
46. Ibid., *Old Comrades Association Gazette*, no. 6 (December 1920): 2.
47. Ibid., *Old Comrades Association Gazette* 6, no. 5 (November 1925): 3.
48. Ibid., *Old Comrades Association Gazette* 8, no. 7 (January 1928): 1.
49. Ibid., *Old Comrades Association Gazette* 12, no. 1 (July 1930): 1.

50. Nora Barker, IWM Sound Archive, Cat No 9731, copyright IWM.

51. IWM, E.J. 1027, *Old Comrades Association Gazette* 13 no.6 (December 1931): 1.

52. Colonel Julia Cowper, *A Short History of the Queen Mary's Army Auxiliary Corps* (Aldershot: Women's Royal Army Corps Association, 1967).

53. IWM, E.J. 1027, *Old Comrades Association Gazette* 3, no. 11 (May 1923): 1.

54. Ibid., *Old Comrades Association Gazette* 6, no. 1 (July 1925): 4. Used by kind permission of the WRAC Association.

55. Ibid., *Old Comrades Association Gazette* 6, no. 9 (March 1926): 1.

56. National Army Museum (NAM), 9811-58, *File of papers on the incorporation of a memorial window to officers and members of the Women's Army Auxiliary Corps in Guildford Cathedral, 1955–1957, Letter from Miss E. Iredale, Sec. of Guildford New Cathedral Fund to Director of WRAC*, 18 October 1955.

57. Ibid.

58. Nora Barker, IWM Sound Archive, Cat No 9731, copyright IWM.

Bibliography

Archival Sources

The National Archives
Air Force Records (AIR10)
Board of Trade Records (BT31)
Cabinet Office Records (CAB17, CAB24)
Ministry of National Service Records (NATS1)
Ministry of Pensions and National Insurance Records (PIN13, PIN15)
Treasury Records (T1)
War Office Records (WO32, WO33, WO95, WO162)

National Army Museum
Women's Royal Army Corps Collection – transferred from the WRAC Museum, Guildford after closure in 1992.

Imperial War Museum
Art Section
Documents and Sound Section
Museum Archive
Women's Work Collection (Army 3, Army 12)

Hull History Centre
Winifred Holtby Collection

Official Publications and Parliamentary Papers
Hansard, House of Commons, 5ᵗʰ Series 1 December–12 December 1919, Vol. 122, Oral Answers.
Hansard, House of Commons, 5ᵗʰ Series 10 February–27 February 1920, Vol. 125, Oral Answers.
The War Office. *The Army Act, 1881, and Certain Other Statutes Relating to the Army. Together with Rules of Procedure, 1881, and Rules for Summary Punishment*. London: HMSO, 1881.
The War Office. *Regulations for the Queen Mary's Army Auxiliary Corps 1918*. London: HMSO, 1918.

The War Office. *Statistics of the Military Effort of the British Empire during the Great War, 1914–20*. London: HMSO, 1922.

Books

Aldington, Richard. *Death of a Hero*. London, Chatto & Windus, 1929.

Anderson, Agnes, ed. *"Johnnie" of QMAAC*. London: Heath Cranton, 1920.

Anonymous. *The Letters of Thomasina Atkins: Private W.A.A.C. on Active Service*. New York: George H. Doran, 1918.

Anonymous. *WAAC: The Woman's Story of the War*. London: T. Werner Laurie Ltd, 1930.

Barton, Edith and Cody, Marguerite. *Eve In Khaki*. London, Edinburgh, New York: Thomas Nelson & Sons Ltd, 1918.

Bidwell, Shelford. *The Women's Royal Army Corps*. London: Leo Cooper Ltd, 1977.

Brittain, Vera. *Testament of Friendship: The Story of Winifred Holtby*. London: Macmillan, 1940.

Carey, Mabel Colebrooke. *Princess Mary: A Biography*. London: Nisbet & Co. Ltd, 1922.

Cowper, Colonel Julia. *A Short History of the Queen Mary's Army Auxiliary Corps*. Aldershot: Women's Royal Army Corps Association, 1967.

Grindlay, I, 3617. *Ripples from the Ranks of the Q.M.A.A.C.* London: Erskine Macdonald Ltd, 1918.

Gwynne-Vaughan, Helen. *Service with the Army*. London: Hutchinson, 1942.

Hall, Radclyffe. *The Well of Loneliness*. London: Jonathan Cape, 1928.

Holtby, Winifred, *Letters to a Friend*. London: Collins, 1937.

Jesse, Fryniwyd Tennyson. *The Sword of Deborah*. New York: George H. Doran, 1919.

Marchant, Bessie. *A Transport Girl in France: A Story of the Adventures of a WAAC*. London: Blackie & Son Ltd, 1919.

Marwick, Arthur. *Women at War, 1914–1918*. London: Fontana, 1977.

Smith, Helen Zenna. *Not So Quiet: Stepdaughters of War*. London: A.E. Marriott, 1930.

Smith, Helen Zenna. *Not So Quiet: Stepdaughters of War*. New York: The Feminist Press, 1989.

Terry, Roy. *Women in Khaki: The Story of the British Woman Soldier*. London: Columbus Books, 1988.

Tweedie, Ethel (Mrs Alec Tweedie). *Women and Soldiers*. London: John Lane, 1918.

Newspapers and Magazines

Aberdeen Daily Journal
Birmingham Daily Post
Daily Mirror
Edinburgh Evening News
Evening Telegraph and Post, Dundee
Hastings and St. Leonards Observer
Illustrated London News
Liverpool Daily Post and Mercury

Liverpool Echo
Manchester Evening News
Motherwell Times
The Times
Yorkshire Evening Post
Miscellaneous
Commonwealth War Graves Commission (CWGC). *Women's Army Auxiliary Corps and Queen Mary's Army Auxiliary Corps, Commonwealth War Graves Commission Casualty Report 1916–1921.*

Recommended Further Reading

Adie, Kate. *Corsets to Camouflage: Women and War.* London: Hodder & Stoughton, 2003.

Condell, Diana and Jean Liddiard. *Working for Victory: Images of Women in the First World War, 1914 – 1918.* London: Routledge & Kegan Paul, 1987.

Crosthwait, Elizabeth. "'The Girl Behind the Man Behind the Gun': The Women's Army Auxiliary Corps, 1914–18." In *Our Work, Our Lives, Our Words: Women's History and Women's Work* edited by Leonore Davidoff and Belinda Westover. London: Macmillan Education Ltd, 1986.

Fountain, Nigel. *Voices from the Twentieth Century: Women at War.* London: Michael O'Mara Books Ltd, 2002.

Gould, Jenny. "Women's Military Services in First World War Britain" in *Behind the Lines: Gender and the Two World Wars* edited by Margaret Higonnet. New Haven and London: Yale University Press, 1987.

Grayzel, Susan. *Women's Identities at War: Gender, Motherhood and Politics in Britain and France during the First World War.* North Carolina: University of North Carolina Press, 1999.

Izzard, Molly. *A Heroine in Her Time: A Life of Dame Helen Gwynne-Vaughan 1879– 1967.* London: Macmillan & Co. Ltd, 1969.

Mitchell, David. *Women on the Warpath: The Story of the Women of the First World War.* London: Jonathan Cape, 1966.

Noakes, Lucy. *Women in the British Army: War and the Gentle Sex, 1907 – 1948.* Abingdon, New York: Routledge, 2006.

Shaw, Diana. "The Forgotten Army of Women: The Overseas Service of the Queen Mary's Army Auxiliary Corps with the British Forces 1917–1921" in *Facing Armageddon* edited by Hugh Cecil and Peter Liddle. Barnsley: Pen & Sword Books Ltd, 1996.

Shipton, Elisabeth. *Female Tommies: The Frontline Women of the First World War.* Stroud: The History Press, 2014.

Storey, Neil and Molly Housego. *Women in the First World War.* Oxford: Shire, 2010.

The National Archives holds the WAAC service records at WO398. Many of the records were severely damaged during a German air raid in September 1940 and records for approximately 7,000 of the women remain.

Index